My PECS
School to Home
Communicator

If Lost Return To:

Name: _____

Address: _____

_____

Parents: _____

_____

Phone: _____

Phone: _____

Cell: _____

Emergency: _____

School: _____

_____

Teacher: _____

Classroom: _____

www.AutismShopper.com

created by
Laura Behrendt © 2007
using Boardmaker Symbols ©
Mayer-Johnson, 1981-2007
All rights reserved worldwide
Used with permission

ISBN 978-0-6151-8289-6

date

month / day / year

_____

What classes did I have?

☐ reading 	☐ math 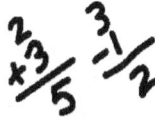	☐ writing 
☐ spelling 	☐ gym 	☐ art 
☐ music 	☐ workbook 	☐

Do I have homework?

☐ yes

☐ no

Comments:

_____

_____

_____

Did I like my lunch?

☐ yummy    ☐ yucky

I ate:

_____

_____

_____

How was my mood today?

☐	happy	☐	sad	☐	frustrated

☐	okay	☐	tired	☐	grumpy

Comments:

_____

_____

_____

_____

_____

_____

_____

_____

_____

Remember: (to take home, bring tomorrow, coming event)

_____

_____

_____

date

month / day / year

_____

What classes did I have?

☐ reading

☐ math

☐ writing

☐ spelling

☐ gym

☐ art

☐ music

☐ workbook

☐

Do I have homework?

☐ yes

☐ no

Comments:

_____
_____
_____

Did I like my lunch?

☐ yummy

☐ yucky

I ate:

_____
_____
_____

How was my mood today?

☐ happy	☐ sad	☐ frustrated
☐ okay	☐ tired	☐ grumpy

Comments:

_____

_____

_____

_____

_____

_____

_____

_____

_____

Remember: (to take home, bring tomorrow, coming event)

_____

_____

_____

date

☐ month / day / year

_____

What classes did I have?

☐ reading

☐ math

☐ writing

☐ spelling
Cat
Ca

☐ gym

☐ art

☐ music

☐ workbook

☐

Do I have homework?

☐ yes

Comments:

_____

☐ no

_____

_____

Did I like my lunch?

☐ yummy

☐ yucky

I ate:

_____

_____

_____

How was my mood today?

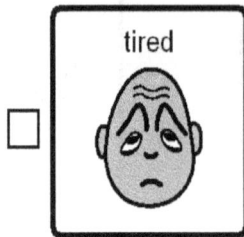

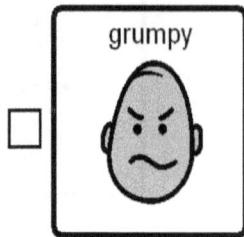

	happy		sad		frustrated
☐		☐		☐	

	okay		tired		grumpy
☐		☐		☐	

Comments:

_____

_____

_____

_____

_____

_____

_____

_____

Remember: (to take home, bring tomorrow, coming event)

_____

_____

_____

date

month / day / year

_____

What classes did I have?

☐ reading

☐ math

☐ writing

☐ spelling   Cat   Ca

☐ gym

☐ art

☐ music

☐ workbook

☐

Do I have homework?

☐ yes

☐ no

Comments:

_____
_____
_____

Did I like my lunch?

☐ yummy

☐ yucky

I ate:

_____
_____
_____

How was my mood today?

☐ happy	☐ sad	☐ frustrated

☐ okay	☐ tired	☐ grumpy

Comments:

_____

_____

_____

_____

_____

_____

_____

_____

Remember: (to take home, bring tomorrow, coming event)

_____

_____

_____

date

month / day / year

_____

What classes did I have?

☐ reading

☐ math

☐ writing

☐ spelling Cat Ca

☐ gym

☐ art

☐ music

☐ workbook

☐

Do I have homework?

☐ yes

☐ no

Comments:

_____

_____

_____

Did I like my lunch?

☐ yummy

☐ yucky

I ate:

_____

_____

_____

How was my mood today?

☐ happy	☐ sad	☐ frustrated
☐ okay	☐ tired	☐ grumpy

Comments:

_____

_____

_____

_____

_____

_____

_____

_____

_____

Remember: (to take home, bring tomorrow, coming event)

_____

_____

_____

date

month / day / year

_____

What classes did I have?

☐ reading

☐ math
$$\begin{array}{c}2\\+3\\\hline 5\end{array} \quad \begin{array}{c}3\\-1\\\hline 2\end{array}$$

☐ writing

☐ spelling
Ca Cat

☐ gym

☐ art

☐ music

☐ workbook

☐

Do I have homework?

☐ yes

Comments:

_____

☐ no

_____

_____

Did I like my lunch?

I ate:

☐ yummy

☐ yucky

_____

_____

_____

How was my mood today?

	happy		sad		frustrated
☐		☐		☐	

	okay		tired		grumpy
☐		☐		☐	

Comments:

_____

_____

_____

_____

_____

_____

_____

_____

_____

Remember: (to take home, bring tomorrow, coming event)

_____

_____

_____

date

month / day / year

_____

What classes did I have?

☐ reading

☐ math

☐ writing

☐ spelling — Ca / Cat

☐ gym

☐ art

☐ music

☐ workbook

☐

Do I have homework?

☐ yes

☐ no

Comments:

_____
_____
_____

Did I like my lunch?

☐ yummy

☐ yucky

I ate:

_____
_____
_____

How was my mood today?

☐	happy
☐	sad
☐	frustrated
☐	okay
☐	tired
☐	grumpy

Comments:

_____

_____

_____

_____

_____

_____

_____

_____

_____

Remember: (to take home, bring tomorrow, coming event)

_____

_____

_____

date

month / day / year

_____

What classes did I have?

reading	math	writing
□	□	□

spelling	gym	art
□	□	□

music	workbook	
□	□	□

Do I have homework?

□ yes   **Comments:**

_____

□ no   _____

_____

Did I like my lunch?

I ate:

□ yummy   □ yucky

_____

_____

_____

How was my mood today?

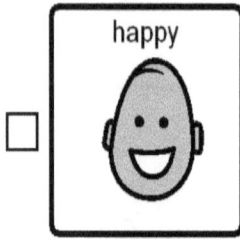

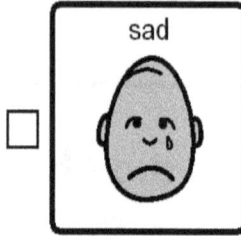

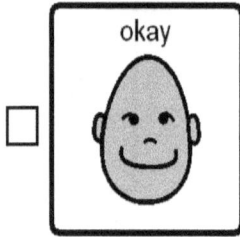

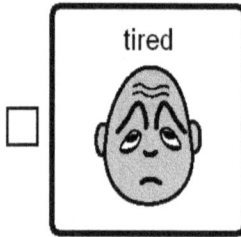

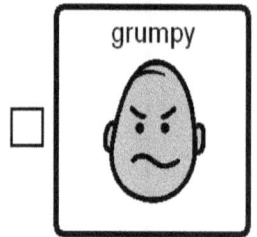

☐ happy	☐ sad	☐ frustrated
☐ okay	☐ tired	☐ grumpy

Comments:

_____

_____

_____

_____

_____

_____

_____

_____

_____

Remember: (to take home, bring tomorrow, coming event)

_____

_____

_____

_____

What classes did I have?

☐ reading

☐ math
$$\frac{\begin{array}{r}2\\+3\end{array}}{5} \quad \frac{\begin{array}{r}3\\-1\end{array}}{2}$$

☐ writing

☐ spelling
Ca Cat

☐ gym

☐ art

☐ music

☐ workbook

☐

Do I have homework?

☐ yes

Comments:

_____

☐ no

_____

_____

Did I like my lunch?

I ate:

☐ yummy

☐ yucky

_____

_____

_____

How was my mood today?

	happy		sad		frustrated
☐		☐		☐	

	okay		tired		grumpy
☐		☐		☐	

Comments:

_____

_____

_____

_____

_____

_____

_____

_____

_____

Remember: (to take home, bring tomorrow, coming event)

_____

_____

_____

_____

What classes did I have?

☐ reading

☐ math

☐ writing

☐ spelling   Cat   Ca

☐ gym

☐ art

☐ music

☐ workbook

☐

Do I have homework?

☐ yes

Comments:

_____

☐ no

_____

_____

Did I like my lunch?

I ate:

☐ yummy

☐ yucky

_____

_____

_____

How was my mood today?

☐ happy	☐ sad	☐ frustrated
☐ okay	☐ tired	☐ grumpy

Comments:

_____

_____

_____

_____

_____

_____

_____

_____

_____

Remember: (to take home, bring tomorrow, coming event)

_____

_____

_____

date

month / day / year

_____

What classes did I have?

☐ reading

☐ math

☐ writing

☐ spelling

☐ gym

☐ art

☐ music

☐ workbook

☐

Do I have homework?

☐ yes

☐ no

Comments:

_____

_____

_____

Did I like my lunch?

☐ yummy

☐ yucky

I ate:

_____

_____

_____

How was my mood today?

☐ happy	☐ sad	☐ frustrated
☐ okay	☐ tired	☐ grumpy

Comments:

_____

_____

_____

_____

_____

_____

_____

_____

_____

Remember: (to take home, bring tomorrow, coming event)

_____

_____

_____

date
month / day / year

_____

What classes did I have?

☐ reading

☐ math

☐ writing

☐ spelling (Ca → Cat)

☐ gym

☐ art

☐ music

☐ workbook

☐

Do I have homework?

☐ yes

☐ no

Comments:

_____

_____

_____

Did I like my lunch?

☐ yummy

☐ yucky

I ate:

_____

_____

_____

How was my mood today?

☐ happy	☐ sad	☐ frustrated
☐ okay	☐ tired	☐ grumpy

Comments:

_____

_____

_____

_____

_____

_____

_____

_____

Remember: (to take home, bring tomorrow, coming event)

_____

_____

_____

date

month / day / year

_____

What classes did I have?

☐ reading

☐ math

☐ writing

☐ spelling
Cat
Ca

☐ gym

☐ art

☐ music

☐ workbook

☐

Do I have homework?

☐ yes

☐ no

Comments:

_____

_____

_____

Did I like my lunch?

☐ yummy

☐ yucky

I ate:

_____

_____

_____

How was my mood today?

	happy		sad		frustrated
☐		☐		☐	

	okay		tired		grumpy
☐		☐		☐	

Comments:

_____

_____

_____

_____

_____

_____

_____

_____

_____

Remember: (to take home, bring tomorrow, coming event)

_____

_____

_____

date

month / day / year

_____

What classes did I have?

| ☐ | reading  | ☐ | math 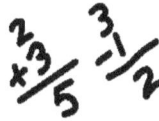 | ☐ | writing  |

| ☐ | spelling  | ☐ | gym  | ☐ | art  |

| ☐ | music  | ☐ | workbook  | ☐ | |

Do I have homework?

☐ yes

☐ no

Comments:

_____

_____

_____

Did I like my lunch?

☐ yummy  ☐ yucky

I ate:

_____

_____

_____

How was my mood today?

	happy		sad		frustrated
☐		☐		☐	

	okay		tired		grumpy
☐		☐		☐	

Comments:

_____

_____

_____

_____

_____

_____

_____

_____

Remember: (to take home, bring tomorrow, coming event)

_____

_____

_____

date

month / day / year

_____

What classes did I have?

reading	math	writing
☐	☐	☐

spelling	gym	art
☐	☐	☐

music	workbook	
☐	☐	☐

Do I have homework?

☐ yes   Comments:

_____

☐ no

_____

_____

Did I like my lunch?

I ate:

☐ yummy   ☐ yucky

_____

_____

_____

How was my mood today?

☐ happy	☐ sad	☐ frustrated
☐ okay	☐ tired	☐ grumpy

Comments:

_____

_____

_____

_____

_____

_____

_____

_____

_____

Remember: (to take home, bring tomorrow, coming event)

_____

_____

_____

date

month / day / year

_____

What classes did I have?

☐ reading	☐ math	☐ writing
☐ spelling — Cat / Ca	☐ gym	☐ art
☐ music	☐ workbook	☐

Do I have homework?

☐ yes

☐ no

Comments:

_____

_____

_____

Did I like my lunch?

☐ yummy

☐ yucky

I ate:

_____

_____

_____

How was my mood today?

☐ happy

☐ sad

☐ frustrated

☐ okay

☐ tired

☐ grumpy

Comments:

_____

_____

_____

_____

_____

_____

_____

_____

_____

Remember: (to take home, bring tomorrow, coming event)

_____

_____

_____

date

month / day / year

_____

What classes did I have?

☐ reading

☐ math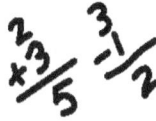

☐ writing

☐ spelling

☐ gym

☐ art

☐ music

☐ workbook

☐

Do I have homework?

☐ yes

☐ no

Comments:

_____

_____

_____

Did I like my lunch?

☐ yummy    ☐ yucky

I ate:

_____

_____

_____

How was my mood today?

☐ happy

☐ sad

☐ frustrated

☐ okay

☐ tired

☐ grumpy

Comments:

_____

_____

_____

_____

_____

_____

_____

_____

_____

Remember: (to take home, bring tomorrow, coming event)

_____

_____

_____

_____

What classes did I have?

☐ reading

☐ math
2
+3
___
5

3
-1/2

☐ writing

☐ spelling
Ca
Cat

☐ gym

☐ art

☐ music

☐ workbook

☐

Do I have homework?

☐ yes

☐ no

Comments:

_____

_____

_____

Did I like my lunch?

☐ yummy

☐ yucky

I ate:

_____

_____

_____

How was my mood today?

☐ **happy**

☐ **sad**

☐ **frustrated**

☐ **okay**

☐ **tired**

☐ **grumpy**

Comments:

_____

_____

_____

_____

_____

_____

_____

_____

_____

Remember: (to take home, bring tomorrow, coming event)

_____

_____

_____

date

month / day / year

_____

What classes did I have?

☐ reading

☐ math

☐ writing

☐ spelling — Cat / Ca

☐ gym

☐ art

☐ music

☐ workbook

☐

Do I have homework?

☐ yes

☐ no

Comments:

_____
_____
_____

Did I like my lunch?

☐ yummy

☐ yucky

I ate:

_____
_____
_____

How was my mood today?

☐	happy	☐	sad	☐	frustrated
☐	okay	☐	tired	☐	grumpy

Comments:

_____

_____

_____

_____

_____

_____

_____

_____

_____

Remember: (to take home, bring tomorrow, coming event)

_____

_____

_____

date

month / day / year

_____

What classes did I have?

☐ reading

☐ math
$$\begin{array}{r} 2 \\ +3 \\ \hline 5 \end{array} \quad \begin{array}{r} 3 \\ -1\frac{1}{2} \end{array}$$

☐ writing

☐ spelling
Cat
Ca

☐ gym

☐ art

☐ music

☐ workbook

☐

Do I have homework?

☐ yes

Comments:

_____

☐ no

_____

_____

Did I like my lunch?

I ate:

☐ yummy

☐ yucky

_____

_____

_____

How was my mood today?

	happy		sad		frustrated
☐		☐		☐	

	okay		tired		grumpy
☐		☐		☐	

Comments:

_____

_____

_____

_____

_____

_____

_____

_____

Remember: (to take home, bring tomorrow, coming event)

_____

_____

_____

date

month / day / year

_____

What classes did I have?

reading	math	writing
☐	☐	☐

$$\begin{array}{c}2\\+3\\\hline 5\end{array} \qquad \begin{array}{c}3\\-1\\\hline 2\end{array}$$

spelling	gym	art
☐ Cat / Ca	☐	☐

music	workbook	
☐	☐	☐

Do I have homework?

☐ yes

☐ no

Comments:

_____

_____

_____

Did I like my lunch?

I ate:

☐ yummy

☐ yucky

_____

_____

_____

How was my mood today?

☐ happy	☐ sad	☐ frustrated
☐ okay	☐ tired	☐ grumpy

Comments:

_____

_____

_____

_____

_____

_____

_____

_____

_____

Remember: (to take home, bring tomorrow, coming event)

_____

_____

_____

date

month / day / year

_____

What classes did I have?

☐ reading

☐ math

☐ writing

☐ spelling

☐ gym

☐ art

☐ music

☐ workbook

☐

Do I have homework?

☐ yes

☐ no

Comments:

_____

_____

_____

Did I like my lunch?

☐ yummy

☐ yucky

I ate:

_____

_____

_____

How was my mood today?

	happy		sad		frustrated
☐	😄	☐	😢	☐	😠

	okay		tired		grumpy
☐	🙂	☐	😩	☐	😠

Comments:

_____

_____

_____

_____

_____

_____

_____

_____

_____

Remember: (to take home, bring tomorrow, coming event)

_____

_____

_____

date

month / day / year

_____

What classes did I have?

☐ reading

☐ math

☐ writing

☐ spelling
Cat
Ca

☐ gym

☐ art

☐ music

☐ workbook

☐

Do I have homework?

☐ yes

☐ no

Comments:

_____

_____

_____

Did I like my lunch?

☐ yummy

☐ yucky

I ate:

_____

_____

_____

How was my mood today?

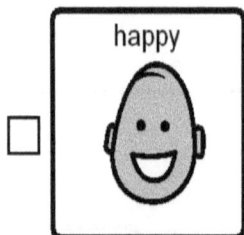

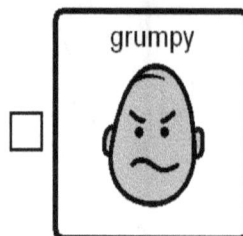

happy	sad	frustrated
☐	☐	☐

okay	tired	grumpy
☐	☐	☐

Comments:

_____

_____

_____

_____

_____

_____

_____

_____

Remember: (to take home, bring tomorrow, coming event)

_____

_____

_____

date

month / day / year

_____

What classes did I have?

☐ reading

☐ math

☐ writing

☐ spelling Cat Ca

☐ gym

☐ art

☐ music

☐ workbook

☐

Do I have homework?

☐ yes

Comments:

_____

_____

☐ no

_____

Did I like my lunch?

I ate:

☐ yummy

☐ yucky

_____

_____

_____

How was my mood today?

☐ happy	☐ sad	☐ frustrated
☐ okay	☐ tired	☐ grumpy

Comments:

_____

_____

_____

_____

_____

_____

_____

_____

_____

Remember: (to take home, bring tomorrow, coming event)

_____

_____

_____

_____

What classes did I have?

☐ reading

☐ math

☐ writing

☐ spelling
Cat
Ca

☐ gym

☐ art

☐ music

☐ workbook

☐

Do I have homework?

☐ yes

☐ no

Comments:

_____

_____

_____

Did I like my lunch?

☐ yummy

☐ yucky

I ate:

_____

_____

_____

How was my mood today?

☐	**happy**
☐	**sad**
☐	**frustrated**
☐	**okay**
☐	**tired**
☐	**grumpy**

Comments:

_____

_____

_____

_____

_____

_____

_____

_____

_____

Remember: (to take home, bring tomorrow, coming event)

_____

_____

_____

_____

What classes did I have?

☐ reading

☐ math

☐ writing

☐ spelling — Cat — Ca

☐ gym

☐ art

☐ music

☐ workbook

☐

Do I have homework?

☐ yes

Comments:

_____

☐ no

_____

_____

Did I like my lunch?

I ate:

☐ yummy

☐ yucky

_____

_____

_____

How was my mood today?

☐ happy	☐ sad	☐ frustrated
☐ okay	☐ tired	☐ grumpy

Comments:

_____

_____

_____

_____

_____

_____

_____

_____

Remember: (to take home, bring tomorrow, coming event)

_____

_____

_____

date

month / day / year

_____

What classes did I have?

☐ **reading**

☐ **math**
2
+3
___
5

3
-1
___
2

☐ **writing**

☐ **spelling**
Cat
Ca

☐ **gym**

☐ **art**

☐ **music**

☐ **workbook**

☐

Do I have homework?

☐ yes

☐ no

Comments:

_____

_____

_____

Did I like my lunch?

☐ yummy

☐ yucky

I ate:

_____

_____

_____

How was my mood today?

	happy		sad		frustrated
☐		☐		☐	

	okay		tired		grumpy
☐		☐		☐	

Comments:

_____

_____

_____

_____

_____

_____

_____

_____

_____

Remember: (to take home, bring tomorrow, coming event)

_____

_____

_____

date

month / day / year

_____

What classes did I have?

☐ reading

☐ math

☐ writing

☐ spelling — Ca / Cat

☐ gym

☐ art

☐ music

☐ workbook

☐

Do I have homework?

☐ yes

☐ no

Comments:

_____

_____

_____

Did I like my lunch?

☐ yummy ☐ yucky

I ate:

_____

_____

_____

How was my mood today?

☐ happy	☐ sad	☐ frustrated
☐ okay	☐ tired	☐ grumpy

Comments:

_____

_____

_____

_____

_____

_____

_____

_____

_____

Remember: (to take home, bring tomorrow, coming event)

_____

_____

_____

date

month / day / year

_____

What classes did I have?

- [ ] reading
- [ ] math
- [ ] writing
- [ ] spelling
- [ ] gym
- [ ] art
- [ ] music
- [ ] workbook
- [ ]

Do I have homework?

- [ ] yes

Comments:

_____

- [ ] no

_____

_____

Did I like my lunch?

I ate:

- [ ] yummy
- [ ] yucky

_____

_____

_____

How was my mood today?

☐ happy

☐ sad

☐ frustrated

☐ okay

☐ tired

☐ grumpy

Comments:

_____

_____

_____

_____

_____

_____

_____

_____

_____

Remember: (to take home, bring tomorrow, coming event)

_____

_____

_____

date

month / day / year

_____

What classes did I have?

☐ reading

☐ math

☐ writing

☐ spelling
Cat
Ca

☐ gym

☐ art

☐ music

☐ workbook

☐

Do I have homework?

☐ yes

☐ no

Comments:

_____

_____

_____

Did I like my lunch?

☐ yummy

☐ yucky

I ate:

_____

_____

_____

How was my mood today?

	happy		sad		frustrated
☐		☐		☐	

	okay		tired		grumpy
☐		☐		☐	

Comments:

_____

_____

_____

_____

_____

_____

_____

_____

Remember: (to take home, bring tomorrow, coming event)

_____

_____

_____

date		
month	day	year

_____

What classes did I have?

☐ reading

☐ math

☐ writing

☐ spelling

☐ gym

☐ art

☐ music

☐ workbook

☐

Do I have homework?

☐ yes

☐ no

Comments:

_____

_____

_____

Did I like my lunch?

☐ yummy

☐ yucky

I ate:

_____

_____

_____

How was my mood today?

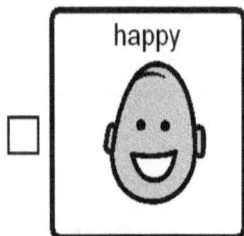

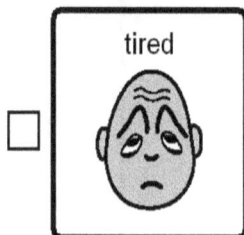

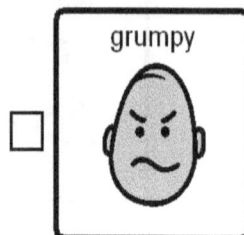

☐	**happy**
☐	**sad**
☐	**frustrated**
☐	**okay**
☐	**tired**
☐	**grumpy**

Comments:

_____

_____

_____

_____

_____

_____

_____

_____

_____

Remember: (to take home, bring tomorrow, coming event)

_____

_____

_____

date

month / day / year

_____

What classes did I have?

☐ reading

☐ math
$$\frac{\overset{2}{+3}}{5} \quad \frac{\overset{3}{-1}}{2}$$

☐ writing

☐ spelling
Ca — Cat

☐ gym

☐ art

☐ music

☐ workbook

☐

Do I have homework?

☐ yes

Comments:

_____

☐ no

_____

_____

Did I like my lunch?

I ate:

☐ yummy

☐ yucky

_____

_____

_____

How was my mood today?

☐ happy	☐ sad	☐ frustrated
☐ okay	☐ tired	☐ grumpy

Comments:

_____

_____

_____

_____

_____

_____

_____

_____

_____

Remember: (to take home, bring tomorrow, coming event)

_____

_____

_____

_____

What classes did I have?

☐ reading

☐ math

☐ writing

☐ spelling
Cat
Ca

☐ gym

☐ art

☐ music

☐ workbook

☐

Do I have homework?

☐ yes

☐ no

Comments:

_____

_____

_____

Did I like my lunch?

☐ yummy

☐ yucky

I ate:

_____

_____

_____

How was my mood today?

	happy		sad		frustrated
☐		☐		☐	

	okay		tired		grumpy
☐		☐		☐	

Comments:

_____

_____

_____

_____

_____

_____

_____

_____

_____

Remember: (to take home, bring tomorrow, coming event)

_____

_____

_____

date

month / day / year

_____

What classes did I have?

☐ reading

☐ math

☐ writing

☐ spelling — Cat / Ca

☐ gym

☐ art

☐ music

☐ workbook

☐

Do I have homework?

☐ yes

☐ no

Comments:

_____

_____

_____

Did I like my lunch?

☐ yummy

☐ yucky

I ate:

_____

_____

_____

How was my mood today?

	happy		sad		frustrated
☐		☐		☐	

	okay		tired		grumpy
☐		☐		☐	

Comments:

_____

_____

_____

_____

_____

_____

_____

_____

_____

Remember: (to take home, bring tomorrow, coming event)

_____

_____

_____

date

month / day / year

_____

What classes did I have?

☐ **reading**

☐ **math**
2
+3
___
5

3
-1½

☐ **writing**

☐ **spelling**
Cat
Ca

☐ **gym**

☐ **art**

☐ **music**

☐ **workbook**

☐

Do I have homework?

☐ **yes**

Comments:

_____

_____

☐ **no**

_____

Did I like my lunch?

I ate:

☐ **yummy**

☐ **yucky**

_____

_____

_____

How was my mood today?

	happy		sad		frustrated
☐		☐		☐	

	okay		tired		grumpy
☐		☐		☐	

Comments:

_____

_____

_____

_____

_____

_____

_____

_____

_____

Remember: (to take home, bring tomorrow, coming event)

_____

_____

_____

date
month / day / year

_____

What classes did I have?

□ reading

□ math

□ writing

□ spelling (Ca / Cat)

□ gym

□ art

□ music

□ workbook

□

Do I have homework?

□ yes

□ no

Comments:

_____

_____

_____

Did I like my lunch?

□ yummy

□ yucky

I ate:

_____

_____

_____

How was my mood today?

	happy		sad		frustrated
☐		☐		☐	

	okay		tired		grumpy
☐		☐		☐	

Comments:

_____

_____

_____

_____

_____

_____

_____

_____

Remember: (to take home, bring tomorrow, coming event)

_____

_____

_____

date
month / day / year

_____

What classes did I have?

☐ reading

☐ math

☐ writing

☐ spelling
Cat
Ca

☐ gym

☐ art

☐ music

☐ workbook

☐

Do I have homework?

☐ yes

☐ no

Comments:

_____
_____
_____

Did I like my lunch?

☐ yummy

☐ yucky

I ate:

_____
_____
_____

How was my mood today?

☐ happy	☐ sad	☐ frustrated
☐ okay	☐ tired	☐ grumpy

Comments:

_____

_____

_____

_____

_____

_____

_____

_____

_____

Remember: (to take home, bring tomorrow, coming event)

_____

_____

_____

date

month / day / year

_____

What classes did I have?

☐ reading

☐ math

☐ writing

☐ spelling — Cat / Ca

☐ gym

☐ art

☐ music

☐ workbook

☐

Do I have homework?

☐ yes

Comments:

_____

_____

☐ no

_____

Did I like my lunch?

☐ yummy

☐ yucky

I ate:

_____

_____

_____

How was my mood today?

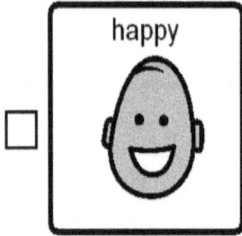

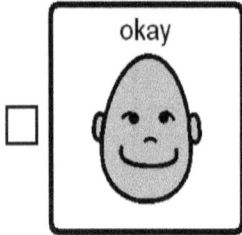

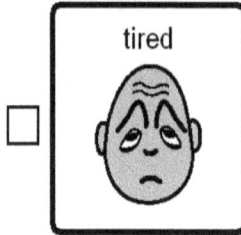

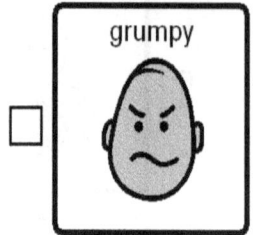

☐	happy
☐	sad
☐	frustrated
☐	okay
☐	tired
☐	grumpy

Comments:

_____

_____

_____

_____

_____

_____

_____

_____

Remember: (to take home, bring tomorrow, coming event)

_____

_____

_____

_____

What classes did I have?

☐ **reading**

☐ **math**

☐ **writing**

☐ **spelling** Cat / Ca

☐ **gym**

☐ **art**

☐ **music**

☐ **workbook**

☐

Do I have homework?

☐ **yes**

Comments:

_____

☐ **no**

_____

_____

Did I like my lunch?

I ate:

☐ **yummy**

☐ **yucky**

_____

_____

_____

How was my mood today?

☐	happy	☐	sad	☐	frustrated
☐	okay	☐	tired	☐	grumpy

Comments:

_____

_____

_____

_____

_____

_____

_____

_____

Remember: (to take home, bring tomorrow, coming event)

_____

_____

_____

_____

What classes did I have?

☐ reading

☐ math
$$\begin{array}{r} 2 \\ +3 \\ \hline 5 \end{array} \qquad \begin{array}{r} 3 \\ -1 \\ \hline 2 \end{array}$$

☐ writing

☐ spelling
Cat
Ca

☐ gym

☐ art

☐ music

☐ workbook

☐

Do I have homework?

☐ yes

Comments:

_____

☐ no

_____

_____

Did I like my lunch?

☐ yummy

☐ yucky

I ate:

_____

_____

_____

How was my mood today?

	happy		sad		frustrated
☐		☐		☐	

	okay		tired		grumpy
☐		☐		☐	

Comments:

_____

_____

_____

_____

_____

_____

_____

_____

_____

Remember: (to take home, bring tomorrow, coming event)

_____

_____

_____

date

month / day / year

_____

What classes did I have?

☐ reading

☐ math

$$\begin{array}{r} 2 \\ +3 \\ \hline 5 \end{array} \qquad \begin{array}{r} 3 \\ -1 \\ \hline 2 \end{array}$$

☐ writing

☐ spelling

Cat

Ca

☐ gym

☐ art

☐ music

☐ workbook

☐

Do I have homework?

☐ yes

Comments:

_____

☐ no

_____

_____

Did I like my lunch?

I ate:

☐ yummy

☐ yucky

_____

_____

_____

How was my mood today?

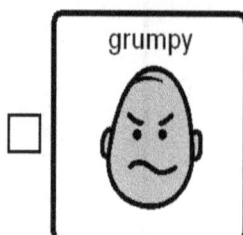

	happy		sad		frustrated
☐		☐		☐	

	okay		tired		grumpy
☐		☐		☐	

Comments:

_____

_____

_____

_____

_____

_____

_____

_____

_____

Remember: (to take home, bring tomorrow, coming event)

_____

_____

_____

date

month / day / year

_____

What classes did I have?

☐ reading

☐ math

☐ writing

☐ spelling — Cat / Ca

☐ gym

☐ art

☐ music

☐ workbook

☐

Do I have homework?

☐ yes

☐ no

Comments:

_____

_____

_____

Did I like my lunch?

☐ yummy

☐ yucky

I ate:

_____

_____

_____

How was my mood today?

☐	happy
☐	sad
☐	frustrated
☐	okay
☐	tired
☐	grumpy

Comments:

_____

_____

_____

_____

_____

_____

_____

_____

_____

Remember: (to take home, bring tomorrow, coming event)

_____

_____

_____

date

month / day / year

_____

What classes did I have?

☐ reading

☐ math

☐ writing

☐ spelling
Cat
Ca

☐ gym

☐ art

☐ music

☐ workbook

☐

Do I have homework?

☐ yes

☐ no

Comments:

_____

_____

_____

Did I like my lunch?

☐ yummy

☐ yucky

I ate:

_____

_____

_____

How was my mood today?

☐ happy	☐ sad	☐ frustrated
☐ okay	☐ tired	☐ grumpy

Comments:

_____

_____

_____

_____

_____

_____

_____

_____

_____

Remember: (to take home, bring tomorrow, coming event)

_____

_____

_____

date

month / day / year

_____

What classes did I have?

☐ reading

☐ math

☐ writing

☐ spelling
Cat
Ca

☐ gym

☐ art

☐ music

☐ workbook

☐

Do I have homework?

☐ yes

☐ no

Comments:

_____
_____
_____

Did I like my lunch?

☐ yummy

☐ yucky

I ate:

_____
_____
_____

How was my mood today?

☐ happy	☐ sad	☐ frustrated
☐ okay	☐ tired	☐ grumpy

Comments:

_____

_____

_____

_____

_____

_____

_____

_____

_____

Remember: (to take home, bring tomorrow, coming event)

_____

_____

_____

date

month / day / year

_____

What classes did I have?

☐ reading

☐ math

☐ writing

☐ spelling Cat Ca

☐ gym

☐ art

☐ music

☐ workbook

☐

Do I have homework?

☐ yes

☐ no

Comments:

_____

_____

_____

Did I like my lunch?

☐ yummy

☐ yucky

I ate:

_____

_____

_____

How was my mood today?

☐ happy	☐ sad	☐ frustrated
☐ okay	☐ tired	☐ grumpy

Comments:

_____

_____

_____

_____

_____

_____

_____

_____

_____

Remember: (to take home, bring tomorrow, coming event)

_____

_____

_____

_____

What classes did I have?

- [ ] reading
- [ ] math
- [ ] writing
- [ ] spelling (Cat / Ca)
- [ ] gym
- [ ] art
- [ ] music
- [ ] workbook
- [ ]

Do I have homework?

- [ ] yes

Comments:

_____

- [ ] no

_____

_____

Did I like my lunch?

- [ ] yummy
- [ ] yucky

I ate:

_____

_____

_____

How was my mood today?

	happy		sad		frustrated
☐		☐		☐	

	okay		tired		grumpy
☐		☐		☐	

Comments:

_____

_____

_____

_____

_____

_____

_____

_____

Remember: (to take home, bring tomorrow, coming event)

_____

_____

_____

date

month / day / year

_____

What classes did I have?

☐ **reading**

☐ **math**

$$2 + 3 = 5$$ $$3 - 1 = 2$$

☐ **writing**

☐ **spelling**

Ca → Cat

☐ **gym**

☐ **art**

☐ **music**

☐ **workbook**

☐

Do I have homework?

☐ **yes**

☐ **no**

Comments:

_____

_____

_____

Did I like my lunch?

☐ **yummy**

☐ **yucky**

I ate:

_____

_____

_____

How was my mood today?

☐ happy	☐ sad	☐ frustrated
☐ okay	☐ tired	☐ grumpy

Comments:

_____

_____

_____

_____

_____

_____

_____

_____

Remember: (to take home, bring tomorrow, coming event)

_____

_____

_____

_____

What classes did I have?

☐ reading

☐ math

☐ writing

☐ spelling
Cat
Ca

☐ gym

☐ art

☐ music

☐ workbook

☐

Do I have homework?

☐ yes

☐ no

Comments:

_____

_____

_____

Did I like my lunch?

☐ yummy

☐ yucky

I ate:

_____

_____

_____

How was my mood today?

☐ happy	☐ sad	☐ frustrated
☐ okay	☐ tired	☐ grumpy

Comments:

_____

_____

_____

_____

_____

_____

_____

_____

_____

Remember: (to take home, bring tomorrow, coming event)

_____

_____

_____

date

month / day / year

_____

What classes did I have?

☐ reading

☐ math

☐ writing

☐ spelling (Cat) Ca

☐ gym

☐ art

☐ music

☐ workbook

☐

Do I have homework?

☐ yes

☐ no

Comments:

_____

_____

Did I like my lunch?

☐ yummy

☐ yucky

I ate:

_____

_____

_____

How was my mood today?

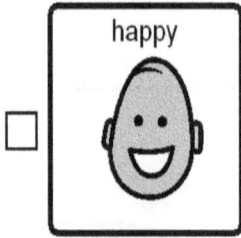

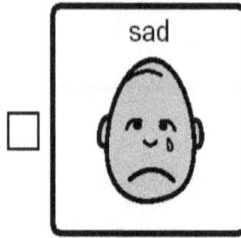

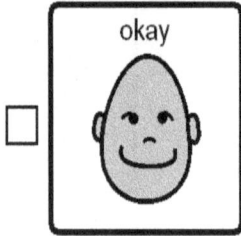

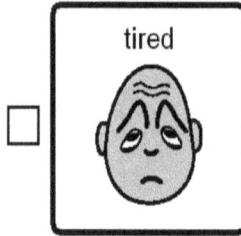

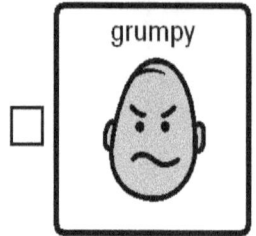

☐	happy
☐	sad
☐	frustrated
☐	okay
☐	tired
☐	grumpy

Comments:

_____

_____

_____

_____

_____

_____

_____

_____

Remember: (to take home, bring tomorrow, coming event)

_____

_____

_____

date
month / day / year

_____

What classes did I have?

☐ reading

☐ math

☐ writing

☐ spelling — Cat

☐ gym

☐ art

☐ music

☐ workbook

☐

Do I have homework?

☐ yes

☐ no

Comments:

_____

_____

_____

Did I like my lunch?

☐ yummy

☐ yucky

I ate:

_____

_____

_____

How was my mood today?

☐ happy	☐ sad	☐ frustrated
☐ okay	☐ tired	☐ grumpy

Comments:

_____

_____

_____

_____

_____

_____

_____

_____

Remember: (to take home, bring tomorrow, coming event)

_____

_____

_____

date

month / day / year

_____

What classes did I have?

☐ reading

☐ math

☐ writing

☐ spelling

☐ gym

☐ art

☐ music

☐ workbook

☐

Do I have homework?

☐ yes

☐ no

Comments:

_____

_____

_____

Did I like my lunch?

☐ yummy

☐ yucky

I ate:

_____

_____

_____

How was my mood today?

☐ happy	☐ sad	☐ frustrated
☐ okay	☐ tired	☐ grumpy

Comments:

_____

_____

_____

_____

_____

_____

_____

_____

_____

Remember: (to take home, bring tomorrow, coming event)

_____

_____

_____

_____

What classes did I have?

☐ reading

☐ math

☐ writing

☐ spelling

☐ gym

☐ art

☐ music

☐ workbook

☐

Do I have homework?

☐ yes

Comments:

_____

_____

☐ no

_____

Did I like my lunch?

I ate:

☐ yummy

☐ yucky

_____

_____

_____

How was my mood today?

	happy		sad		frustrated
☐		☐		☐	

	okay		tired		grumpy
☐		☐		☐	

Comments:

_____

_____

_____

_____

_____

_____

_____

_____

Remember: (to take home, bring tomorrow, coming event)

_____

_____

_____

date

month / day / year

_____

What classes did I have?

☐ reading

☐ math

2
+3
—
5

3
−1
—
2

☐ writing

☐ spelling

Cat

Ca

☐ gym

☐ art

☐ music

☐ workbook

☐

Do I have homework?

☐ yes

Comments:

_____

☐ no

X

_____

_____

Did I like my lunch?

I ate:

☐ yummy

☐ yucky

_____

_____

_____

How was my mood today?

☐	happy	☐	sad	☐	frustrated
☐	okay	☐	tired	☐	grumpy

Comments:

_____

_____

_____

_____

_____

_____

_____

_____

_____

Remember: (to take home, bring tomorrow, coming event)

_____

_____

_____

_____

What classes did I have?

☐ reading

☐ math

☐ writing

☐ spelling
Cat
Ca

☐ gym

☐ art

☐ music

☐ workbook

☐

Do I have homework?

☐ yes

Comments:

_____

☐ no

_____

_____

Did I like my lunch?

I ate:

☐ yummy

☐ yucky

_____

_____

_____

How was my mood today?

☐ happy	☐ sad	☐ frustrated
☐ okay	☐ tired	☐ grumpy

Comments:

_____

_____

_____

_____

_____

_____

_____

_____

Remember: (to take home, bring tomorrow, coming event)

_____

_____

_____

date

month / day / year

_____

What classes did I have?

☐ reading

☐ math

☐ writing

☐ spelling
Cat
Ca

☐ gym

☐ art

☐ music

☐ workbook

☐

Do I have homework?

☐ yes

☐ no

Comments:

_____

_____

_____

Did I like my lunch?

☐ yummy

☐ yucky

I ate:

_____

_____

_____

How was my mood today?

☐ happy	☐ sad	☐ frustrated
☐ okay	☐ tired	☐ grumpy

Comments:

_____

_____

_____

_____

_____

_____

_____

_____

_____

Remember: (to take home, bring tomorrow, coming event)

_____

_____

_____

date

month / day / year

_____

What classes did I have?

☐ reading

☐ math

☐ writing

☐ spelling — Cat / Ca

☐ gym

☐ art

☐ music

☐ workbook

☐

Do I have homework?

☐ yes

Comments:

_____

☐ no

_____

_____

Did I like my lunch?

I ate:

☐ yummy

☐ yucky

_____

_____

_____

How was my mood today?

☐ happy	☐ sad	☐ frustrated
☐ okay	☐ tired	☐ grumpy

Comments:

_____

_____

_____

_____

_____

_____

_____

_____

_____

Remember: (to take home, bring tomorrow, coming event)

_____

_____

_____

date

month / day / year

_____

What classes did I have?

☐ reading

☐ math

☐ writing

☐ spelling Ca Cat

☐ gym

☐ art

☐ music

☐ workbook

☐

Do I have homework?

☐ yes

☐ no

Comments:

_____

_____

_____

Did I like my lunch?

☐ yummy

☐ yucky

I ate:

_____

_____

_____

How was my mood today?

	happy		sad		frustrated
☐		☐		☐	

	okay		tired		grumpy
☐		☐		☐	

Comments:

_____

_____

_____

_____

_____

_____

_____

_____

Remember: (to take home, bring tomorrow, coming event)

_____

_____

_____

date

month / day / year

_____

What classes did I have?

☐ reading

☐ math

☐ writing

☐ spelling

☐ gym

☐ art

☐ music

☐ workbook

☐

Do I have homework?

☐ yes

☐ no

Comments:

_____

_____

_____

Did I like my lunch?

☐ yummy

☐ yucky

I ate:

_____

_____

_____

How was my mood today?

☐ **happy**

☐ **sad**

☐ **frustrated**

☐ **okay**

☐ **tired**

☐ **grumpy**

Comments:

_____

_____

_____

_____

_____

_____

_____

_____

_____

Remember: (to take home, bring tomorrow, coming event)

_____

_____

_____

date

month / day / year

_____

What classes did I have?

☐ reading

☐ math

☐ writing

☐ spelling — Cat / Ca

☐ gym

☐ art

☐ music

☐ workbook

☐

Do I have homework?

☐ yes

☐ no

Comments:

_____

_____

_____

Did I like my lunch?

☐ yummy

☐ yucky

I ate:

_____

_____

_____

How was my mood today?

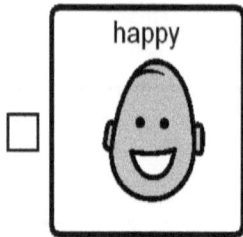

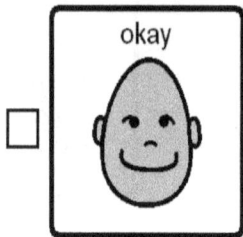

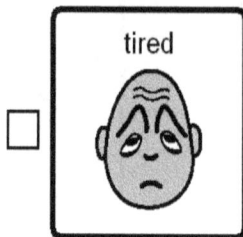

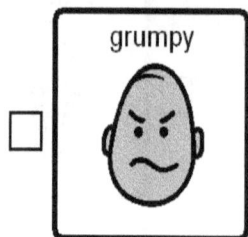

	happy		sad		frustrated
☐		☐		☐	

	okay		tired		grumpy
☐		☐		☐	

Comments:

_____

_____

_____

_____

_____

_____

_____

_____

_____

_____

Remember: (to take home, bring tomorrow, coming event)

_____

_____

_____

_____

What classes did I have?

☐ reading

☐ math

☐ writing

☐ spelling   Cat   Ca

☐ gym

☐ art

☐ music

☐ workbook

☐

Do I have homework?

☐ yes

☐ no

Comments:

_____

_____

_____

Did I like my lunch?

☐ yummy

☐ yucky

I ate:

_____

_____

_____

How was my mood today?

☐ happy	☐ sad	☐ frustrated
☐ okay	☐ tired	☐ grumpy

Comments:

_____

_____

_____

_____

_____

_____

_____

_____

Remember: (to take home, bring tomorrow, coming event)

_____

_____

_____

date

month / day / year

_____

What classes did I have?

☐ reading

☐ math

☐ writing

☐ spelling — Cat — Ca

☐ gym

☐ art

☐ music

☐ workbook

☐

Do I have homework?

☐ yes

☐ no

Comments:

_____

_____

_____

Did I like my lunch?

☐ yummy

☐ yucky

I ate:

_____

_____

_____

How was my mood today?

☐ happy

☐ sad

☐ frustrated

☐ okay

☐ tired

☐ grumpy

Comments:

_____

_____

_____

_____

_____

_____

_____

_____

Remember: (to take home, bring tomorrow, coming event)

_____

_____

_____

date

month / day / year

_____

What classes did I have?

☐ reading

☐ math

☐ writing

☐ spelling

☐ gym

☐ art

☐ music

☐ workbook

☐

Do I have homework?

☐ yes

☐ no

Comments:

_____

_____

_____

Did I like my lunch?

☐ yummy

☐ yucky

I ate:

_____

_____

_____

How was my mood today?

☐ happy	☐ sad	☐ frustrated
☐ okay	☐ tired	☐ grumpy

Comments:

_____

_____

_____

_____

_____

_____

_____

_____

Remember: (to take home, bring tomorrow, coming event)

_____

_____

_____

_____

What classes did I have?

☐ reading

☐ math

☐ writing

☐ spelling
Cat
Ca

☐ gym

☐ art

☐ music

☐ workbook

☐

Do I have homework?

☐ yes

☐ no

Comments:

_____

_____

_____

Did I like my lunch?

I ate:

☐ yummy

☐ yucky

_____

_____

_____

How was my mood today?

☐ happy	☐ sad	☐ frustrated
☐ okay	☐ tired	☐ grumpy

Comments:

_____

_____

_____

_____

_____

_____

_____

_____

_____

Remember: (to take home, bring tomorrow, coming event)

_____

_____

_____

date

month / day / year

_____

What classes did I have?

☐ reading

☐ math

☐ writing

☐ spelling

☐ gym

☐ art

☐ music

☐ workbook

☐

Do I have homework?

☐ yes

☐ no

Comments:

_____
_____
_____

Did I like my lunch?

☐ yummy

☐ yucky

I ate:

_____
_____
_____

How was my mood today?

☐ happy	☐ sad	☐ frustrated
☐ okay	☐ tired	☐ grumpy

Comments:

_____

_____

_____

_____

_____

_____

_____

_____

_____

Remember: (to take home, bring tomorrow, coming event)

_____

_____

_____

date

month / day / year

_____

What classes did I have?

☐ reading

☐ math
$$\begin{array}{r} 2 \\ +3 \\ \hline 5 \end{array} \qquad \begin{array}{r} 3 \\ -1 \\ \hline 2 \end{array}$$

☐ writing

☐ spelling
Ca — Cat

☐ gym

☐ art

☐ music

☐ workbook

☐

Do I have homework?

☐ yes

☐ no

Comments:

_____

_____

_____

Did I like my lunch?

☐ yummy   ☐ yucky

I ate:

_____

_____

_____

How was my mood today?

	happy		sad		frustrated
☐		☐		☐	

	okay		tired		grumpy
☐		☐		☐	

Comments:

_____

_____

_____

_____

_____

_____

_____

_____

_____

Remember: (to take home, bring tomorrow, coming event)

_____

_____

_____

date

month / day / year

_____

What classes did I have?

☐ reading

☐ math

☐ writing

☐ spelling
Cat
Ca

☐ gym

☐ art

☐ music

☐ workbook

☐

Do I have homework?

☐ yes

☐ no

Comments:

_____

_____

_____

Did I like my lunch?

☐ yummy

☐ yucky

I ate:

_____

_____

_____

How was my mood today?

☐ happy	☐ sad	☐ frustrated
☐ okay	☐ tired	☐ grumpy

Comments:

_____

_____

_____

_____

_____

_____

_____

_____

Remember: (to take home, bring tomorrow, coming event)

_____

_____

_____

date

month / day / year

_____

What classes did I have?

☐ reading

☐ math

☐ writing

☐ spelling   Cat   Ca

☐ gym

☐ art

☐ music

☐ workbook

☐

Do I have homework?

☐ yes

Comments:

_____

☐ no

_____

_____

Did I like my lunch?

☐ yummy

☐ yucky

I ate:

_____

_____

_____

How was my mood today?

☐ happy	☐ sad	☐ frustrated
☐ okay	☐ tired	☐ grumpy

Comments:

_____

_____

_____

_____

_____

_____

_____

_____

_____

Remember: (to take home, bring tomorrow, coming event)

_____

_____

_____

date

month / day / year

_____

What classes did I have?

☐ reading

☐ math

☐ writing

☐ spelling
Cat
Ca

☐ gym

☐ art

☐ music

☐ workbook

☐

Do I have homework?

☐ yes

☐ no

Comments:

_____
_____
_____

Did I like my lunch?

☐ yummy

☐ yucky

I ate:

_____
_____
_____

How was my mood today?

| ☐ happy | ☐ sad | ☐ frustrated |
| ☐ okay | ☐ tired | ☐ grumpy |

Comments:

_____

_____

_____

_____

_____

_____

_____

_____

Remember: (to take home, bring tomorrow, coming event)

_____

_____

_____

date

month / day / year

_____

What classes did I have?

☐ reading

☐ math

☐ writing

☐ spelling — Cat — Ca

☐ gym

☐ art

☐ music

☐ workbook

☐

Do I have homework?

☐ yes

☐ no

Comments:

_____

_____

_____

Did I like my lunch?

☐ yummy

☐ yucky

I ate:

_____

_____

_____

How was my mood today?

☐ happy	☐ sad	☐ frustrated
☐ okay	☐ tired	☐ grumpy

Comments:

_____

_____

_____

_____

_____

_____

_____

_____

_____

Remember: (to take home, bring tomorrow, coming event)

_____

_____

_____

date

month / day / year

_____

What classes did I have?

☐ reading

☐ math
$$\begin{array}{r} 2 \\ +3 \\ \hline 5 \end{array} \qquad \begin{array}{r} 3 \\ -1 \\ \hline 2 \end{array}$$

☐ writing

☐ spelling
Cat
Ca

☐ gym

☐ art

☐ music

☐ workbook

☐

Do I have homework?

☐ yes

☐ no

Comments:

_____

_____

_____

Did I like my lunch?

☐ yummy

☐ yucky

I ate:

_____

_____

_____

How was my mood today?

☐ happy	☐ sad	☐ frustrated
☐ okay	☐ tired	☐ grumpy

Comments:

_____

_____

_____

_____

_____

_____

_____

_____

_____

Remember: (to take home, bring tomorrow, coming event)

_____

_____

_____

date

month / day / year

_____

What classes did I have?

☐ reading

☐ math

☐ writing

☐ spelling — Cat / Ca

☐ gym

☐ art

☐ music

☐ workbook

☐

Do I have homework?

☐ yes

☐ no

Comments:

_____

_____

_____

Did I like my lunch?

☐ yummy

☐ yucky

I ate:

_____

_____

_____

How was my mood today?

- [ ] happy
- [ ] sad
- [ ] frustrated
- [ ] okay
- [ ] tired
- [ ] grumpy

Comments:

_____

_____

_____

_____

_____

_____

_____

_____

_____

Remember: (to take home, bring tomorrow, coming event)

_____

_____

_____

_____

What classes did I have?

☐ reading

☐ math

☐ writing

☐ spelling

☐ gym

☐ art

☐ music

☐ workbook

☐

Do I have homework?

☐ yes

☐ no

Comments:

_____

_____

_____

Did I like my lunch?

☐ yummy

☐ yucky

I ate:

_____

_____

_____

How was my mood today?

☐ happy	☐ sad	☐ frustrated
☐ okay	☐ tired	☐ grumpy

Comments:

_____

_____

_____

_____

_____

_____

_____

_____

_____

Remember: (to take home, bring tomorrow, coming event)

_____

_____

_____

date

month / day / year

_____

What classes did I have?

☐ reading

☐ math

☐ writing

☐ spelling — Cat — Ca

☐ gym

☐ art

☐ music

☐ workbook

☐

Do I have homework?

☐ yes

☐ no

Comments:

_____

_____

_____

Did I like my lunch?

☐ yummy

☐ yucky

I ate:

_____

_____

_____

How was my mood today?

☐ happy	☐ sad	☐ frustrated
☐ okay	☐ tired	☐ grumpy

Comments:

_____

_____

_____

_____

_____

_____

_____

_____

Remember: (to take home, bring tomorrow, coming event)

_____

_____

_____

date

month / day / year

_____

What classes did I have?

☐ reading

☐ math

☐ writing

☐ spelling — Ca / Cat

☐ gym

☐ art

☐ music

☐ workbook

☐

Do I have homework?

☐ yes

☐ no

Comments:

_____

_____

_____

Did I like my lunch?

☐ yummy

☐ yucky

I ate:

_____

_____

_____

How was my mood today?

☐	happy	☐	sad	☐	frustrated
☐	okay	☐	tired	☐	grumpy

Comments:

_____

_____

_____

_____

_____

_____

_____

_____

_____

Remember: (to take home, bring tomorrow, coming event)

_____

_____

_____

date

month / day / year

_____

What classes did I have?

☐ reading

☐ math

☐ writing

☐ spelling Cat Ca

☐ gym

☐ art

☐ music

☐ workbook

☐

Do I have homework?

☐ yes

☐ no

Comments:

_____

_____

_____

Did I like my lunch?

☐ yummy

☐ yucky

I ate:

_____

_____

_____

How was my mood today?

- [ ] happy
- [ ] sad
- [ ] frustrated
- [ ] okay
- [ ] tired
- [ ] grumpy

Comments:

_____

_____

_____

_____

_____

_____

_____

_____

Remember: (to take home, bring tomorrow, coming event)

_____

_____

_____

date

month / day / year

_____

What classes did I have?

☐ **reading**

☐ **math**

☐ **writing**

☐ **spelling** Cat / Ca

☐ **gym**

☐ **art**

☐ **music**

☐ **workbook**

☐

Do I have homework?

☐ **yes**

☐ **no** ✗

Comments:

_____
_____
_____

Did I like my lunch?

☐ **yummy**

☐ **yucky**

I ate:

_____
_____
_____

How was my mood today?

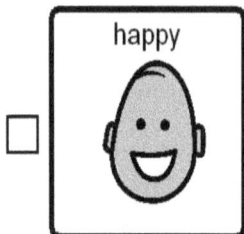

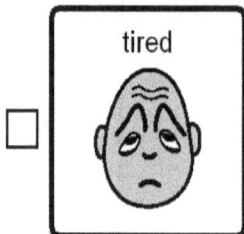

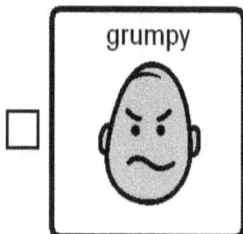

☐ happy

☐ sad

☐ frustrated

☐ okay

☐ tired

☐ grumpy

Comments:

_____

_____

_____

_____

_____

_____

_____

_____

Remember: (to take home, bring tomorrow, coming event)

_____

_____

_____

date

month / day / year

_____

What classes did I have?

☐ reading

☐ math

☐ writing

☐ spelling — Cat / Ca

☐ gym

☐ art

☐ music

☐ workbook

☐

Do I have homework?

☐ yes

☐ no

Comments:

_____

_____

_____

Did I like my lunch?

☐ yummy

☐ yucky

I ate:

_____

_____

_____

How was my mood today?

☐ happy	☐ sad	☐ frustrated
☐ okay	☐ tired	☐ grumpy

Comments:

_____

_____

_____

_____

_____

_____

_____

_____

_____

Remember: (to take home, bring tomorrow, coming event)

_____

_____

_____

date

month / day / year

_____

What classes did I have?

☐ reading

☐ math

$$\begin{array}{r} 2 \\ +3 \\ \hline 5 \end{array} \qquad \begin{array}{r} 3 \\ -1 \\ \hline 2 \end{array}$$

☐ writing

☐ spelling

Ca — Cat

☐ gym

☐ art

☐ music

☐ workbook

☐

Do I have homework?

☐ yes

☐ no

Comments:

_____

_____

_____

Did I like my lunch?

☐ yummy

☐ yucky

I ate:

_____

_____

_____

How was my mood today?

☐ happy	☐ sad	☐ frustrated
☐ okay	☐ tired	☐ grumpy

Comments:

_____

_____

_____

_____

_____

_____

_____

_____

_____

Remember: (to take home, bring tomorrow, coming event)

_____

_____

_____

date

month / day / year

_____

What classes did I have?

☐ reading

☐ math

☐ writing

☐ spelling Ca Cat

☐ gym

☐ art

☐ music

☐ workbook

☐

Do I have homework?

☐ yes

Comments:

_____

_____

☐ no

_____

Did I like my lunch?

I ate:

☐ yummy

☐ yucky

_____

_____

_____

How was my mood today?

happy	sad	frustrated

okay	tired	grumpy

Comments:

_____

_____

_____

_____

_____

_____

_____

_____

_____

Remember: (to take home, bring tomorrow, coming event)

_____

_____

_____

date

month / day / year

_____

What classes did I have?

☐ reading

☐ math

☐ writing

☐ spelling — Ca Cat

☐ gym

☐ art

☐ music

☐ workbook

☐

Do I have homework?

☐ yes

☐ no

Comments:

_____

_____

_____

Did I like my lunch?

☐ yummy

☐ yucky

I ate:

_____

_____

_____

How was my mood today?

	happy		sad		frustrated
☐	😀	☐	😢	☐	😠

	okay		tired		grumpy
☐	🙂	☐	😩	☐	😡

Comments:

_____

_____

_____

_____

_____

_____

_____

_____

_____

Remember: (to take home, bring tomorrow, coming event)

_____

_____

_____

date

month / day / year

_____

What classes did I have?

☐ reading

☐ math

☐ writing

☐ spelling
Cat
Ca

☐ gym

☐ art

☐ music

☐ workbook

☐

Do I have homework?

☐ yes

☐ no

Comments:

_____
_____
_____

Did I like my lunch?

☐ yummy

☐ yucky

I ate:

_____
_____
_____

How was my mood today?

	happy		sad		frustrated
☐	😀	☐	😢	☐	😖

	okay		tired		grumpy
☐	🙂	☐	😪	☐	😠

Comments:

_____

_____

_____

_____

_____

_____

_____

_____

_____

Remember: (to take home, bring tomorrow, coming event)

_____

_____

_____

date

month / day / year

_____

What classes did I have?

☐ reading

☐ math

☐ writing

☐ spelling
Cat
Ca

☐ gym

☐ art

☐ music

☐ workbook

☐

Do I have homework?

☐ yes

☐ no

Comments:

_____

_____

_____

Did I like my lunch?

☐ yummy

☐ yucky

I ate:

_____

_____

_____

How was my mood today?

	happy		sad		frustrated
☐		☐		☐	

	okay		tired		grumpy
☐		☐		☐	

Comments:

_____

_____

_____

_____

_____

_____

_____

_____

_____

Remember: (to take home, bring tomorrow, coming event)

_____

_____

_____

date
month / day / year

_____

What classes did I have?

☐ reading

☐ math
$$\begin{array}{r} 2 \\ +3 \\ \hline 5 \end{array} \quad \begin{array}{r} 3 \\ -1 \\ \hline 2 \end{array}$$

☐ writing

☐ spelling
Ca Cat

☐ gym

☐ art

☐ music

☐ workbook

☐

Do I have homework?

☐ yes

☐ no

Comments:

_____

_____

_____

Did I like my lunch?

☐ yummy

☐ yucky

I ate:

_____

_____

_____

How was my mood today?

	happy		sad		frustrated
☐		☐		☐	

	okay		tired		grumpy
☐		☐		☐	

Comments:

_____

_____

_____

_____

_____

_____

_____

_____

Remember: (to take home, bring tomorrow, coming event)

_____

_____

_____

date

month / day / year

_____

What classes did I have?

☐ reading

☐ math

☐ writing

☐ spelling — Cat / Ca

☐ gym

☐ art

☐ music

☐ workbook

☐

Do I have homework?

☐ yes

☐ no

Comments:

_____

_____

_____

Did I like my lunch?

☐ yummy

☐ yucky

I ate:

_____

_____

_____

How was my mood today?

☐ happy	☐ sad	☐ frustrated
☐ okay	☐ tired	☐ grumpy

Comments:

_____

_____

_____

_____

_____

_____

_____

_____

_____

Remember: (to take home, bring tomorrow, coming event)

_____

_____

_____

date

month / day / year

_____

What classes did I have?

□ reading

□ math

□ writing

□ spelling — Cat, Ca

□ gym

□ art

□ music

□ workbook

□

Do I have homework?

□ yes

□ no

Comments:

_____
_____
_____

Did I like my lunch?

□ yummy

□ yucky

I ate:

_____
_____
_____

How was my mood today?

☐ happy	☐ sad	☐ frustrated
☐ okay	☐ tired	☐ grumpy

Comments:

_____

_____

_____

_____

_____

_____

_____

_____

_____

_____

Remember: (to take home, bring tomorrow, coming event)

_____

_____

_____

date
month / day / year

_____

What classes did I have?

☐ **reading**

☐ **math**
$$\begin{array}{r} 2 \\ +3 \\ \hline 5 \end{array} \qquad \begin{array}{r} 3 \\ -1 \\ \hline 2 \end{array}$$

☐ **writing**

☐ **spelling**
Cat
Ca

☐ **gym**

☐ **art**

☐ **music**

☐ **workbook**

☐

Do I have homework?

☐ **yes**

☐ **no**

Comments:

_____
_____
_____

Did I like my lunch?

☐ **yummy**   ☐ **yucky**

I ate:

_____
_____
_____

How was my mood today?

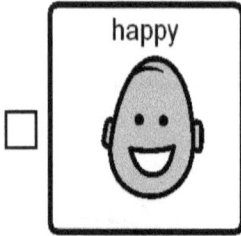

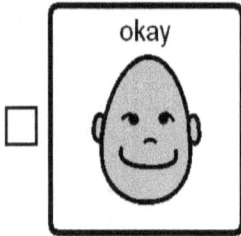

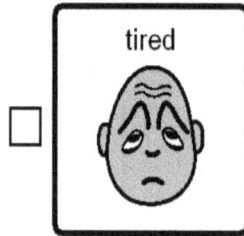

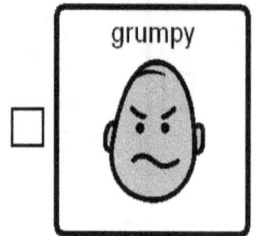

☐ happy	☐ sad	☐ frustrated
☐ okay	☐ tired	☐ grumpy

Comments:

_____

_____

_____

_____

_____

_____

_____

_____

Remember: (to take home, bring tomorrow, coming event)

_____

_____

_____

date

month / day / year

_____

What classes did I have?

☐ reading

☐ math

$\frac{2}{+3}{5}$ $\frac{3}{-1}{2}$

☐ writing

☐ spelling
Cat
Ca

☐ gym

☐ art

☐ music

☐ workbook

☐

Do I have homework?

☐ yes

Comments:

_____

☐ no

_____

_____

Did I like my lunch?

☐ yummy

☐ yucky

I ate:

_____

_____

_____

How was my mood today?

	happy		sad		frustrated
☐		☐		☐	

	okay		tired		grumpy
☐		☐		☐	

Comments:

_____

_____

_____

_____

_____

_____

_____

_____

Remember: (to take home, bring tomorrow, coming event)

_____

_____

_____

date
month / day / year

_____

What classes did I have?

☐ reading

☐ math

☐ writing

☐ spelling

☐ gym

☐ art

☐ music

☐ workbook

☐

Do I have homework?

☐ yes   Comments:

_____

☐ no

_____

_____

Did I like my lunch?

☐ yummy   ☐ yucky

I ate:

_____

_____

_____

How was my mood today?

☐ happy	☐ sad	☐ frustrated
☐ okay	☐ tired	☐ grumpy

Comments:

_____

_____

_____

_____

_____

_____

_____

_____

Remember: (to take home, bring tomorrow, coming event)

_____

_____

_____

date

month / day / year

_____

What classes did I have?

☐ reading

☐ math

☐ writing

☐ spelling — Cat, Ca

☐ gym

☐ art

☐ music

☐ workbook

☐

Do I have homework?

☐ yes

☐ no

Comments:

_____
_____
_____

Did I like my lunch?

☐ yummy

☐ yucky

I ate:

_____
_____
_____

How was my mood today?

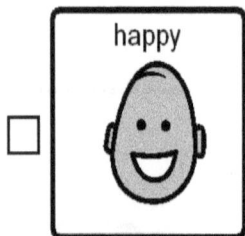

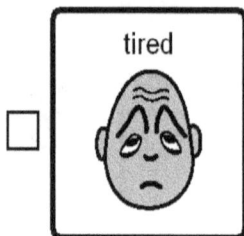

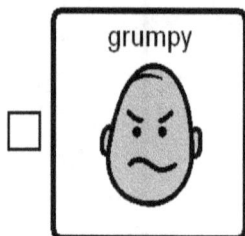

☐ happy	☐ sad	☐ frustrated
☐ okay	☐ tired	☐ grumpy

Comments:

_____

_____

_____

_____

_____

_____

_____

_____

_____

Remember: (to take home, bring tomorrow, coming event)

_____

_____

_____

date

month / day / year

_____

What classes did I have?

☐ reading

☐ math

☐ writing

☐ spelling

Cat

Ca

☐ gym

☐ art

☐ music

☐ workbook

☐

Do I have homework?

☐ yes

Comments:

_____

☐ no

_____

_____

Did I like my lunch?

I ate:

☐ yummy

☐ yucky

_____

_____

_____

How was my mood today?

☐ happy	☐ sad	☐ frustrated
☐ okay	☐ tired	☐ grumpy

Comments:

_____

_____

_____

_____

_____

_____

_____

_____

_____

Remember: (to take home, bring tomorrow, coming event)

_____

_____

_____

date

month / day / year

_____

What classes did I have?

☐ reading

☐ math

☐ writing

☐ spelling — Cat / Ca

☐ gym

☐ art

☐ music

☐ workbook

☐

Do I have homework?

☐ yes

☐ no

Comments:

_____

_____

_____

Did I like my lunch?

☐ yummy

☐ yucky

I ate:

_____

_____

_____

How was my mood today?

☐	happy	☐	sad	☐	frustrated

☐	okay	☐	tired	☐	grumpy

Comments:

_____

_____

_____

_____

_____

_____

_____

_____

Remember: (to take home, bring tomorrow, coming event)

_____

_____

_____

_____

What classes did I have?

☐ reading

☐ math

☐ writing

☐ spelling — Cat Ca

☐ gym

☐ art

☐ music

☐ workbook

☐

Do I have homework?

☐ yes

Comments:

_____

☐ no

_____

_____

Did I like my lunch?

I ate:

☐ yummy

☐ yucky

_____

_____

_____

How was my mood today?

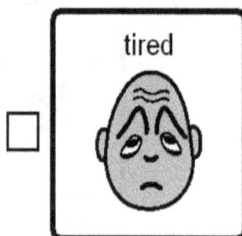

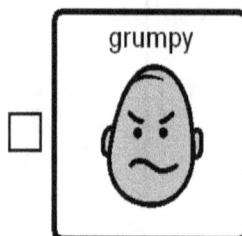

☐ happy	☐ sad	☐ frustrated
☐ okay	☐ tired	☐ grumpy

Comments:

_____

_____

_____

_____

_____

_____

_____

_____

_____

Remember: (to take home, bring tomorrow, coming event)

_____

_____

_____

date

month / day / year

□ _____

What classes did I have?

□ **reading**

□ **math**

□ **writing**

□ **spelling** — Cat — Ca

□ **gym**

□ **art**

□ **music**

□ **workbook**

□

Do I have homework?

□ **yes**

Comments:

_____

□ **no**

_____

_____

Did I like my lunch?

I ate:

□ **yummy**

□ **yucky**

_____

_____

_____

How was my mood today?

☐	happy	☐ sad	☐ frustrated
☐	okay	☐ tired	☐ grumpy

Comments:

_____

_____

_____

_____

_____

_____

_____

_____

Remember: (to take home, bring tomorrow, coming event)

_____

_____

_____

date

month / day / year

_____

What classes did I have?

☐ reading

☐ math

☐ writing

☐ spelling — Ca / Cat

☐ gym

☐ art

☐ music

☐ workbook

☐

Do I have homework?

☐ yes

☐ no

Comments:

_____
_____
_____

Did I like my lunch?

☐ yummy

☐ yucky

I ate:

_____
_____
_____

How was my mood today?

☐ happy	☐ sad	☐ frustrated
☐ okay	☐ tired	☐ grumpy

Comments:

_____

_____

_____

_____

_____

_____

_____

_____

_____

Remember: (to take home, bring tomorrow, coming event)

_____

_____

_____

date

month / day / year

_____

What classes did I have?

☐ reading

☐ math

☐ writing

☐ spelling — Cat / Ca

☐ gym

☐ art

☐ music

☐ workbook

☐

Do I have homework?

☐ yes

Comments:

_____

☐ no

_____

_____

Did I like my lunch?

☐ yummy

☐ yucky

I ate:

_____

_____

_____

How was my mood today?

☐ happy	☐ sad	☐ frustrated
☐ okay	☐ tired	☐ grumpy

Comments:

_____

_____

_____

_____

_____

_____

_____

_____

_____

Remember: (to take home, bring tomorrow, coming event)

_____

_____

_____

date

month / day / year

_____

What classes did I have?

☐ reading

☐ math

☐ writing

☐ spelling
Cat
Ca

☐ gym

☐ art

☐ music

☐ workbook

☐

Do I have homework?

☐ yes

Comments:

_____

☐ no

_____

_____

Did I like my lunch?

I ate:

☐ yummy

☐ yucky

_____

_____

_____

How was my mood today?

| ☐ happy | ☐ sad | ☐ frustrated |
| ☐ okay | ☐ tired | ☐ grumpy |

Comments:

_____

_____

_____

_____

_____

_____

_____

_____

_____

Remember: (to take home, bring tomorrow, coming event)

_____

_____

_____

date
month / day / year

_____

What classes did I have?

reading	math	writing
☐	☐ $\begin{array}{r}2\\+3\\\hline 5\end{array}$ $\begin{array}{r}3\\-1\\\hline 2\end{array}$	☐

spelling	gym	art
☐ Ca (Cat)	☐	☐

music	workbook	
☐	☐	☐

Do I have homework?

☐ yes

Comments:

_____

_____

☐ no

_____

Did I like my lunch?

I ate:

☐ yummy   ☐ yucky

_____

_____

_____

How was my mood today?

☐ happy	☐ sad	☐ frustrated
☐ okay	☐ tired	☐ grumpy

Comments:

_____

_____

_____

_____

_____

_____

_____

_____

Remember: (to take home, bring tomorrow, coming event)

_____

_____

_____

date

month / day / year

_____

What classes did I have?

- [ ] reading
- [ ] math
- [ ] writing
- [ ] spelling (Cat, Ca)
- [ ] gym
- [ ] art
- [ ] music
- [ ] workbook
- [ ]

Do I have homework?

- [ ] yes

Comments:

_____

- [ ] no

_____

_____

Did I like my lunch?

I ate:

- [ ] yummy
- [ ] yucky

_____

_____

_____

How was my mood today?

	happy		sad		frustrated
☐	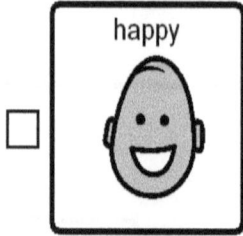	☐		☐	

	okay		tired		grumpy
☐	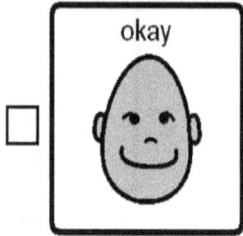	☐		☐	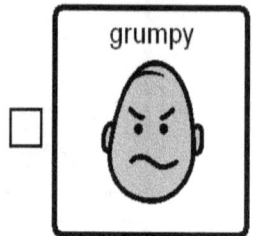

Comments:

_____

_____

_____

_____

_____

_____

_____

_____

_____

Remember: (to take home, bring tomorrow, coming event)

_____

_____

_____

date

month / day / year

_____

What classes did I have?

☐ reading

☐ math

☐ writing

☐ spelling
Cat
Ca

☐ gym

☐ art

☐ music

☐ workbook

☐

Do I have homework?

☐ yes

☐ no

Comments:

_____

_____

_____

Did I like my lunch?

☐ yummy

☐ yucky

I ate:

_____

_____

_____

How was my mood today?

☐ happy	☐ sad	☐ frustrated
☐ okay	☐ tired	☐ grumpy

Comments:

_____

_____

_____

_____

_____

_____

_____

_____

_____

Remember: (to take home, bring tomorrow, coming event)

_____

_____

_____

date

month / day / year

_____

What classes did I have?

☐ reading	☐ math	☐ writing
☐ spelling Cat Ca	☐ gym	☐ art
☐ music	☐ workbook	☐

Do I have homework?

☐ yes

☐ no

Comments:

_____

_____

_____

Did I like my lunch?

☐ yummy ☐ yucky

I ate:

_____

_____

_____

How was my mood today?

☐ happy	☐ sad	☐ frustrated
☐ okay	☐ tired	☐ grumpy

Comments:

_____

_____

_____

_____

_____

_____

_____

_____

_____

Remember: (to take home, bring tomorrow, coming event)

_____

_____

_____

date

month / day / year

_____

What classes did I have?

☐ **reading**

☐ **math**

$$\begin{array}{r} 2 \\ +3 \\ \hline 5 \end{array} \qquad \begin{array}{r} 3 \\ -1 \\ \hline 2 \end{array}$$

☐ **writing**

☐ **spelling**

Cat

Ca

☐ **gym**

☐ **art**

☐ **music**

☐ **workbook**

☐

Do I have homework?

☐ **yes**

☐ **no**

Comments:

_____

_____

_____

Did I like my lunch?

☐ **yummy**

☐ **yucky**

I ate:

_____

_____

_____

How was my mood today?

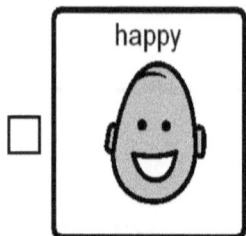

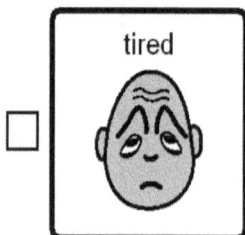

☐ happy	☐ sad	☐ frustrated
☐ okay	☐ tired	☐ grumpy

Comments:

_____

_____

_____

_____

_____

_____

_____

_____

_____

Remember: (to take home, bring tomorrow, coming event)

_____

_____

_____

date
month / day / year

_____

What classes did I have?

☐ reading
☐ math
☐ writing

☐ spelling (Ca → Cat)
☐ gym
☐ art

☐ music
☐ workbook
☐

Do I have homework?

☐ yes
☐ no

Comments:

_____
_____
_____

Did I like my lunch?

☐ yummy
☐ yucky

I ate:

_____
_____
_____

How was my mood today?

	happy		sad		frustrated
☐		☐		☐	

	okay		tired		grumpy
☐		☐		☐	

Comments:

_____

_____

_____

_____

_____

_____

_____

_____

_____

Remember: (to take home, bring tomorrow, coming event)

_____

_____

_____

date

month / day / year

_____

What classes did I have?

☐ reading	☐ math	☐ writing
☐ spelling	☐ gym	☐ art
☐ music	☐ workbook	☐

Do I have homework?

☐ yes   Comments:

_____

☐ no

_____

_____

Did I like my lunch?

I ate:

☐ yummy   ☐ yucky

_____

_____

_____

How was my mood today?

☐ happy	☐ sad	☐ frustrated
☐ okay	☐ tired	☐ grumpy

Comments:

_____

_____

_____

_____

_____

_____

_____

_____

_____

Remember: (to take home, bring tomorrow, coming event)

_____

_____

_____

date

month / day / year

_____

What classes did I have?

☐ reading	☐ math	☐ writing
☐ spelling — Cat / Ca	☐ gym	☐ art
☐ music	☐ workbook	☐

Do I have homework?

☐ yes

☐ no

Comments:

_____

_____

_____

Did I like my lunch?

☐ yummy   ☐ yucky

I ate:

_____

_____

_____

How was my mood today?

☐ happy	☐ sad	☐ frustrated
☐ okay	☐ tired	☐ grumpy

Comments:

_____

_____

_____

_____

_____

_____

_____

_____

_____

Remember: (to take home, bring tomorrow, coming event)

_____

_____

_____

date

month / day / year

_____

What classes did I have?

☐ reading

☐ math

☐ writing

☐ spelling
Cat
Ca

☐ gym

☐ art

☐ music

☐ workbook

☐

Do I have homework?

☐ yes

Comments:

_____

☐ no

_____

_____

Did I like my lunch?

☐ yummy

☐ yucky

I ate:

_____

_____

_____

How was my mood today?

☐ happy	☐ sad	☐ frustrated
☐ okay	☐ tired	☐ grumpy

Comments:

_____

_____

_____

_____

_____

_____

_____

_____

_____

Remember: (to take home, bring tomorrow, coming event)

_____

_____

_____

date

month / day / year

_____

What classes did I have?

☐ reading

☐ math

☐ writing

☐ spelling — Ca Cat

☐ gym

☐ art

☐ music

☐ workbook

☐

Do I have homework?

☐ yes

Comments:

_____

☐ no

_____

_____

Did I like my lunch?

I ate:

☐ yummy

☐ yucky

_____

_____

_____

How was my mood today?

☐ happy	☐ sad	☐ frustrated
☐ okay	☐ tired	☐ grumpy

Comments:

_____

_____

_____

_____

_____

_____

_____

_____

Remember: (to take home, bring tomorrow, coming event)

_____

_____

_____

date

month / day / year

_____

What classes did I have?

☐ reading

☐ math
$$\begin{array}{r} 2 \\ +3 \\ \hline 5 \end{array} \qquad \begin{array}{r} 3 \\ -1 \\ \hline 2 \end{array}$$

☐ writing

☐ spelling
Cat
Ca

☐ gym

☐ art

☐ music

☐ workbook

☐

Do I have homework?

☐ yes

☐ no

Comments:

_____

_____

_____

Did I like my lunch?

☐ yummy

☐ yucky

I ate:

_____

_____

_____

How was my mood today?

☐ happy

☐ sad

☐ frustrated

☐ okay

☐ tired

☐ grumpy

Comments:

_____

_____

_____

_____

_____

_____

_____

_____

_____

Remember: (to take home, bring tomorrow, coming event)

_____

_____

_____

date
month / day / year

_____

What classes did I have?

☐ reading

☐ math

☐ writing

☐ spelling — Cat — Ca

☐ gym

☐ art

☐ music

☐ workbook

☐

Do I have homework?

☐ yes

☐ no

Comments:
_____
_____
_____

Did I like my lunch?

☐ yummy

☐ yucky

I ate:
_____
_____
_____

How was my mood today?

☐	**happy**
☐	**sad**
☐	**frustrated**
☐	**okay**
☐	**tired**
☐	**grumpy**

Comments:

_____

_____

_____

_____

_____

_____

_____

_____

_____

Remember: (to take home, bring tomorrow, coming event)

_____

_____

_____

date
month / day / year

_____

What classes did I have?

☐ reading

☐ math

☐ writing

☐ spelling
Cat
Ca

☐ gym

☐ art

☐ music

☐ workbook

☐

Do I have homework?

☐ yes

Comments:

_____

☐ no

_____

_____

Did I like my lunch?

☐ yummy

☐ yucky

I ate:

_____

_____

_____

How was my mood today?

☐	happy	☐	sad	☐	frustrated
☐	okay	☐	tired	☐	grumpy

Comments:

_____

_____

_____

_____

_____

_____

_____

_____

Remember: (to take home, bring tomorrow, coming event)

_____

_____

_____

date

month / day / year

_____

What classes did I have?

☐ reading

☐ math

2
+3
—
5

3
-1
—
2

☐ writing

☐ spelling

Cat

Ca

☐ gym

☐ art

☐ music

☐ workbook

☐

Do I have homework?

☐ yes

Comments:

_____

☐ no

_____

_____

Did I like my lunch?

I ate:

☐ yummy

☐ yucky

_____

_____

_____

How was my mood today?

☐ happy	☐ sad	☐ frustrated
☐ okay	☐ tired	☐ grumpy

Comments:

_____

_____

_____

_____

_____

_____

_____

_____

_____

Remember: (to take home, bring tomorrow, coming event)

_____

_____

_____

date

month / day / year

_____

What classes did I have?

☐ reading

☐ math

$$\begin{array}{r}2\\+3\\\hline 5\end{array}$$ $$\begin{array}{r}3\\-1\\\hline 2\end{array}$$

☐ writing

☐ spelling — Cat — Ca

☐ gym

☐ art

☐ music

☐ workbook

☐

Do I have homework?

☐ yes

☐ no

Comments:

_____

_____

_____

Did I like my lunch?

☐ yummy

☐ yucky

I ate:

_____

_____

_____

How was my mood today?

	happy		sad		frustrated
☐		☐		☐	

	okay		tired		grumpy
☐		☐		☐	

Comments:

_____

_____

_____

_____

_____

_____

_____

_____

Remember: (to take home, bring tomorrow, coming event)

_____

_____

_____

date

month / day / year

_____

What classes did I have?

- [ ] reading
- [ ] math
- [ ] writing
- [ ] spelling
- [ ] gym
- [ ] art
- [ ] music
- [ ] workbook
- [ ]

Do I have homework?

- [ ] yes
- [ ] no

Comments:

_____

_____

_____

Did I like my lunch?

- [ ] yummy
- [ ] yucky

I ate:

_____

_____

_____

How was my mood today?

	happy		sad		frustrated
☐		☐		☐	

	okay		tired		grumpy
☐		☐		☐	

Comments:

_____

_____

_____

_____

_____

_____

_____

_____

Remember: (to take home, bring tomorrow, coming event)

_____

_____

_____

date

month / day / year

_____

What classes did I have?

☐ reading

☐ math

☐ writing

☐ spelling — Cat, Ca

☐ gym

☐ art

☐ music

☐ workbook

☐

Do I have homework?

☐ yes

☐ no

Comments:

_____
_____
_____

Did I like my lunch?

☐ yummy

☐ yucky

I ate:

_____
_____
_____

How was my mood today?

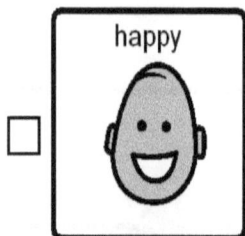

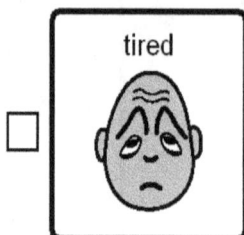

	happy		sad		frustrated
☐		☐		☐	

	okay		tired		grumpy
☐		☐		☐	

Comments:

_____

_____

_____

_____

_____

_____

_____

_____

Remember: (to take home, bring tomorrow, coming event)

_____

_____

_____

_____

What classes did I have?

☐ reading

☐ math
$\frac{\begin{array}{r}2\\+3\end{array}}{5}$ $\frac{\begin{array}{r}3\\-1\end{array}}{2}$

☐ writing

☐ spelling
Cat
Ca

☐ gym

☐ art

☐ music

☐ workbook

☐

Do I have homework?

☐ yes

☐ no

Comments:

_____

_____

_____

Did I like my lunch?

☐ yummy

☐ yucky

I ate:

_____

_____

_____

How was my mood today?

- [ ] happy
- [ ] sad
- [ ] frustrated
- [ ] okay
- [ ] tired
- [ ] grumpy

Comments:

_____
_____
_____
_____
_____
_____
_____
_____
_____

Remember: (to take home, bring tomorrow, coming event)

_____
_____
_____

date

month / day / year

_____

What classes did I have?

☐ reading

☐ math

☐ writing

☐ spelling — Ca Cat

☐ gym

☐ art

☐ music

☐ workbook

☐

Do I have homework?

☐ yes

☐ no

Comments:
_____
_____
_____

Did I like my lunch?

☐ yummy

☐ yucky

I ate:
_____
_____
_____

How was my mood today?

☐ happy	☐ sad	☐ frustrated
☐ okay	☐ tired	☐ grumpy

Comments:

_____

_____

_____

_____

_____

_____

_____

_____

_____

_____

Remember: (to take home, bring tomorrow, coming event)

_____

_____

_____

date

month / day / year

_____

What classes did I have?

	reading		math		writing
☐		☐	2+3/5 3-1/2	☐	

	spelling		gym		art
☐	Ca Cat	☐		☐	

	music		workbook		
☐		☐		☐	

Do I have homework?

☐ yes

Comments:

_____

☐ no

_____

_____

Did I like my lunch?

I ate:

☐ yummy ☐ yucky

_____

_____

_____

How was my mood today?

☐ happy	☐ sad	☐ frustrated
☐ okay	☐ tired	☐ grumpy

Comments:

_____

_____

_____

_____

_____

_____

_____

_____

_____

Remember: (to take home, bring tomorrow, coming event)

_____

_____

_____

date

month / day / year

_____

What classes did I have?

☐ reading

☐ math

☐ writing

☐ spelling — Cat — Ca

☐ gym

☐ art

☐ music

☐ workbook

☐

Do I have homework?

☐ yes

☐ no

Comments:

_____

_____

_____

Did I like my lunch?

☐ yummy

☐ yucky

I ate:

_____

_____

_____

How was my mood today?

☐ happy	☐ sad	☐ frustrated
☐ okay	☐ tired	☐ grumpy

Comments:

_____

_____

_____

_____

_____

_____

_____

_____

_____

Remember: (to take home, bring tomorrow, coming event)

_____

_____

_____

_____

What classes did I have?

	reading
☐	

	math
☐	

	writing
☐	

	spelling
☐	

	gym
☐	

	art
☐	

	music
☐	

	workbook
☐	

☐	

Do I have homework?

☐ yes

☐ no

Comments:

_____

_____

_____

Did I like my lunch?

☐ yummy

☐ yucky

I ate:

_____

_____

_____

How was my mood today?

☐ happy	☐ sad	☐ frustrated
☐ okay	☐ tired	☐ grumpy

Comments:

_____

_____

_____

_____

_____

_____

_____

_____

Remember: (to take home, bring tomorrow, coming event)

_____

_____

_____

date

month / day / year

_____

What classes did I have?

☐ reading

☐ math
$\begin{array}{r} 2 \\ +3 \\ \hline 5 \end{array}$ $\begin{array}{r} 3 \\ -1 \\ \hline 2 \end{array}$

☐ writing

☐ spelling
Cat
Ca

☐ gym

☐ art

☐ music

☐ workbook

☐

Do I have homework?

☐ yes

Comments:
_____
_____
_____

☐ no

Did I like my lunch?

☐ yummy

☐ yucky

I ate:
_____
_____
_____

How was my mood today?

☐ happy

☐ sad

☐ frustrated

☐ okay

☐ tired

☐ grumpy

Comments:

_____

_____

_____

_____

_____

_____

_____

_____

_____

Remember: (to take home, bring tomorrow, coming event)

_____

_____

_____

date

month / day / year

_____

What classes did I have?

☐ reading

☐ math

☐ writing

☐ spelling — Cat — Ca

☐ gym

☐ art

☐ music

☐ workbook

☐

Do I have homework?

☐ yes

Comments:

_____

☐ no

_____

_____

Did I like my lunch?

I ate:

☐ yummy

☐ yucky

_____

_____

_____

How was my mood today?

	happy		sad		frustrated
☐		☐		☐	

	okay		tired		grumpy
☐		☐		☐	

Comments:

_____

_____

_____

_____

_____

_____

_____

_____

Remember: (to take home, bring tomorrow, coming event)

_____

_____

_____

date

month / day / year

_____

What classes did I have?

☐ reading

☐ math

☐ writing

☐ spelling — Ca / Cat

☐ gym

☐ art

☐ music

☐ workbook

☐

Do I have homework?

☐ yes

☐ no

Comments:

_____

_____

_____

Did I like my lunch?

☐ yummy

☐ yucky

I ate:

_____

_____

_____

How was my mood today?

☐	happy
☐	sad
☐	frustrated
☐	okay
☐	tired
☐	grumpy

Comments:

_____

_____

_____

_____

_____

_____

_____

_____

_____

Remember: (to take home, bring tomorrow, coming event)

_____

_____

_____

date

month / day / year

_____

What classes did I have?

	reading		math		writing
☐		☐	$2 + 3 = 5$ $3 - 1\frac{1}{2}$	☐	

	spelling		gym		art
☐	Cat / Ca	☐		☐	

	music		workbook		
☐		☐		☐	

Do I have homework?

☐ yes

☐ no

Comments:

_____

_____

_____

Did I like my lunch?

☐ yummy   ☐ yucky

I ate:

_____

_____

_____

How was my mood today?

☐ happy	☐ sad	☐ frustrated
☐ okay	☐ tired	☐ grumpy

Comments:

_____

_____

_____

_____

_____

_____

_____

_____

_____

Remember: (to take home, bring tomorrow, coming event)

_____

_____

_____

_____

What classes did I have?

☐ **reading**

☐ **math**

☐ **writing**

☐ **spelling**
Ca *Cat*

☐ **gym**

☐ **art**

☐ **music**

☐ **workbook**

☐

Do I have homework?

☐ **yes**

Comments:

_____

☐ **no**

_____

_____

Did I like my lunch?

I ate:

☐ **yummy**

☐ **yucky**

_____

_____

_____

How was my mood today?

- [ ] happy
- [ ] sad
- [ ] frustrated
- [ ] okay
- [ ] tired
- [ ] grumpy

Comments:

_____

_____

_____

_____

_____

_____

_____

_____

Remember: (to take home, bring tomorrow, coming event)

_____

_____

_____

date

month / day / year

_____

What classes did I have?

☐ reading

☐ math

☐ writing

☐ spelling
Cat
Ca

☐ gym

☐ art

☐ music

☐ workbook

☐

Do I have homework?

☐ yes

☐ no

Comments:

_____

_____

_____

Did I like my lunch?

☐ yummy

☐ yucky

I ate:

_____

_____

_____

How was my mood today?

	happy		sad		frustrated
☐		☐		☐	

	okay		tired		grumpy
☐		☐		☐	

Comments:

_____

_____

_____

_____

_____

_____

_____

_____

Remember: (to take home, bring tomorrow, coming event)

_____

_____

_____

date

month / day / year

_____

What classes did I have?

☐ **reading**

☐ **math**
$$\begin{array}{r} 2 \\ +3 \\ \hline 5 \end{array} \qquad \begin{array}{r} 3 \\ -1 \\ \hline 2 \end{array}$$

☐ **writing**

☐ **spelling**
Ca Cat

☐ **gym**

☐ **art**

☐ **music**

☐ **workbook**

☐

Do I have homework?

☐ yes

☐ no

Comments:

_____

_____

_____

Did I like my lunch?

☐ yummy

☐ yucky

I ate:

_____

_____

_____

How was my mood today?

☐ happy

☐ sad

☐ frustrated

☐ okay

☐ tired

☐ grumpy

Comments:

_____

_____

_____

_____

_____

_____

_____

_____

_____

Remember: (to take home, bring tomorrow, coming event)

_____

_____

_____

date

month / day / year

_____

What classes did I have?

☐ reading

☐ math

☐ writing

☐ spelling — Ca "Cat"

☐ gym

☐ art

☐ music

☐ workbook

☐

Do I have homework?

☐ yes

☐ no

Comments:

_____

_____

_____

Did I like my lunch?

☐ yummy

☐ yucky

I ate:

_____

_____

_____

How was my mood today?

	happy		sad		frustrated
☐		☐		☐	

	okay		tired		grumpy
☐		☐		☐	

Comments:

_____

_____

_____

_____

_____

_____

_____

_____

_____

Remember: (to take home, bring tomorrow, coming event)

_____

_____

_____

date

month / day / year

_____

What classes did I have?

☐ **reading**

☐ **math**

☐ **writing**

☐ **spelling**

Cat

Ca

☐ **gym**

☐ **art**

☐ **music**

☐ **workbook**

☐

Do I have homework?

☐ **yes**

Comments:

_____

_____

☐ **no**

_____

Did I like my lunch?

I ate:

☐ **yummy**

☐ **yucky**

_____

_____

_____

How was my mood today?

☐ happy	☐ sad	☐ frustrated
☐ okay	☐ tired	☐ grumpy

Comments:

_____

_____

_____

_____

_____

_____

_____

_____

Remember: (to take home, bring tomorrow, coming event)

_____

_____

_____

date

month / day / year

_____

What classes did I have?

☐ **reading**

☐ **math**

☐ **writing**

☐ **spelling**
Cat
Ca

☐ **gym**

☐ **art**

☐ **music**

☐ **workbook**

☐

Do I have homework?

☐ yes

☐ no

Comments:

_____
_____
_____

Did I like my lunch?

☐ yummy ☐ yucky

I ate:

_____
_____
_____

How was my mood today?

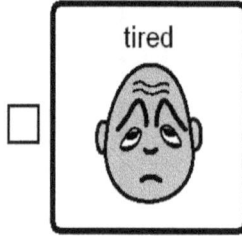

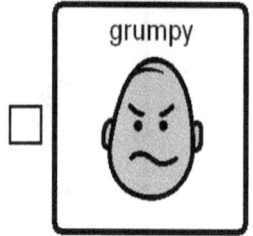

☐ happy	☐ sad	☐ frustrated
☐ okay	☐ tired	☐ grumpy

Comments:

_____

_____

_____

_____

_____

_____

_____

_____

Remember: (to take home, bring tomorrow, coming event)

_____

_____

_____

_____

What classes did I have?

☐ reading

☐ math

☐ writing

☐ spelling — Cat / Ca

☐ gym

☐ art

☐ music

☐ workbook

☐

Do I have homework?

☐ yes

☐ no

Comments:

_____
_____
_____

Did I like my lunch?

☐ yummy

☐ yucky

I ate:

_____
_____
_____

How was my mood today?

☐ happy	☐ sad	☐ frustrated
☐ okay	☐ tired	☐ grumpy

Comments:

_____

_____

_____

_____

_____

_____

_____

_____

Remember: (to take home, bring tomorrow, coming event)

_____

_____

_____

date

month / day / year

_____

What classes did I have?

☐ reading	☐ math	☐ writing
☐ spelling Ca Cat	☐ gym	☐ art
☐ music	☐ workbook	☐

Do I have homework?

☐ yes

☐ no

Comments:

_____

_____

_____

Did I like my lunch?

☐ yummy   ☐ yucky

I ate:

_____

_____

_____

How was my mood today?

☐	happy	☐	sad	☐	frustrated
☐	okay	☐	tired	☐	grumpy

Comments:

_____

_____

_____

_____

_____

_____

_____

_____

Remember: (to take home, bring tomorrow, coming event)

_____

_____

_____

date

month / day / year

_____

What classes did I have?

☐ reading

☐ math
$$2 \atop +3 \over 5$$ $$3 \atop -1 \over 2$$

☐ writing

☐ spelling
Cat
Ca

☐ gym

☐ art

☐ music

☐ workbook

☐

Do I have homework?

☐ yes

☐ no

Comments:

_____
_____
_____

Did I like my lunch?

☐ yummy   ☐ yucky

I ate:

_____
_____
_____

How was my mood today?

☐ happy	☐ sad	☐ frustrated
☐ okay	☐ tired	☐ grumpy

Comments:

_____

_____

_____

_____

_____

_____

_____

_____

_____

Remember: (to take home, bring tomorrow, coming event)

_____

_____

_____

date

month / day / year

_____

What classes did I have?

☐ reading

☐ math

☐ writing

☐ spelling — Cat — Ca

☐ gym

☐ art

☐ music

☐ workbook

☐

Do I have homework?

☐ yes

☐ no

Comments:

_____
_____
_____

Did I like my lunch?

☐ yummy

☐ yucky

I ate:

_____
_____
_____

How was my mood today?

☐ happy

☐ sad

☐ frustrated

☐ okay

☐ tired

☐ grumpy

Comments:

_____

_____

_____

_____

_____

_____

_____

_____

_____

Remember: (to take home, bring tomorrow, coming event)

_____

_____

_____

date

month / day / year

_____

What classes did I have?

☐ reading

☐ math

☐ writing

☐ spelling
Cat
Ca

☐ gym

☐ art

☐ music

☐ workbook

☐

Do I have homework?

☐ yes

☐ no

Comments:

_____

_____

_____

Did I like my lunch?

☐ yummy

☐ yucky

I ate:

_____

_____

_____

How was my mood today?

☐	happy
☐	sad
☐	frustrated
☐	okay
☐	tired
☐	grumpy

Comments:

_____

_____

_____

_____

_____

_____

_____

_____

Remember: (to take home, bring tomorrow, coming event)

_____

_____

_____

date

month / day / year

_____

What classes did I have?

☐ **reading**

☐ **math**
$$\begin{array}{c} 2 \\ +3 \\ \hline 5 \end{array} \quad \begin{array}{c} 3 \\ -1 \\ \hline 2 \end{array}$$

☐ **writing**

☐ **spelling**
Ca → Cat

☐ **gym**

☐ **art**

☐ **music**

☐ **workbook**

☐

Do I have homework?

☐ yes

☐ no

Comments:

_____

_____

_____

Did I like my lunch?

☐ yummy

☐ yucky

I ate:

_____

_____

_____

How was my mood today?

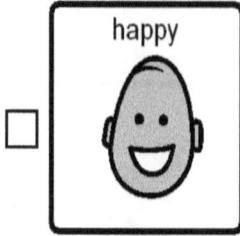

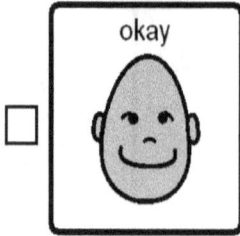

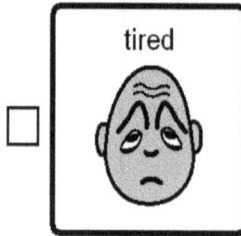

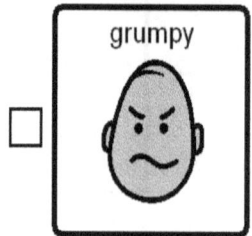

☐ happy

☐ sad

☐ frustrated

☐ okay

☐ tired

☐ grumpy

Comments:

_____

_____

_____

_____

_____

_____

_____

_____

_____

Remember: (to take home, bring tomorrow, coming event)

_____

_____

_____

date

month / day / year

_____

What classes did I have?

☐ reading

☐ math

☐ writing

☐ spelling
Cat
Ca

☐ gym

☐ art

☐ music

☐ workbook

☐

Do I have homework?

☐ yes

☐ no

Comments:

_____
_____
_____

Did I like my lunch?

☐ yummy

☐ yucky

I ate:

_____
_____
_____

How was my mood today?

☐ happy	☐ sad	☐ frustrated
☐ okay	☐ tired	☐ grumpy

Comments:

_____

_____

_____

_____

_____

_____

_____

_____

_____

Remember: (to take home, bring tomorrow, coming event)

_____

_____

_____

date

month / day / year

_____

What classes did I have?

☐ reading

☐ math

☐ writing

☐ spelling
Cat
Ca

☐ gym

☐ art

☐ music

☐ workbook

☐

Do I have homework?

☐ yes

☐ no

Comments:

_____

_____

_____

Did I like my lunch?

☐ yummy

☐ yucky

I ate:

_____

_____

_____

How was my mood today?

☐ happy	☐ sad	☐ frustrated
☐ okay	☐ tired	☐ grumpy

Comments:

_____

_____

_____

_____

_____

_____

_____

_____

_____

Remember: (to take home, bring tomorrow, coming event)

_____

_____

_____

date

month / day / year

_____

What classes did I have?

☐ reading

☐ math
$$\frac{\begin{array}{r}2\\+3\end{array}}{5} \quad \frac{\begin{array}{r}3\\-1\end{array}}{2}$$

☐ writing

☐ spelling
Cat
Ca

☐ gym

☐ art

☐ music

☐ workbook

☐

Do I have homework?

☐ yes

☐ no

Comments:

_____

_____

_____

Did I like my lunch?

☐ yummy

☐ yucky

I ate:

_____

_____

_____

How was my mood today?

☐ happy	
☐ sad	
☐ frustrated	
☐ okay	
☐ tired	
☐ grumpy	

Comments:

_____

_____

_____

_____

_____

_____

_____

_____

Remember: (to take home, bring tomorrow, coming event)

_____

_____

_____

_____

What classes did I have?

☐ reading

☐ math

☐ writing

☐ spelling — Cat — Ca

☐ gym

☐ art

☐ music

☐ workbook

☐

Do I have homework?

☐ yes

☐ no

Comments:

_____
_____
_____

Did I like my lunch?

☐ yummy

☐ yucky

I ate:

_____
_____
_____

How was my mood today?

□ happy

□ sad

□ frustrated

□ okay

□ tired

□ grumpy

Comments:

_____

_____

_____

_____

_____

_____

_____

_____

_____

Remember: (to take home, bring tomorrow, coming event)

_____

_____

_____

date

month / day / year

_____

What classes did I have?

☐	reading	☐	math	☐	writing
☐	spelling Cat Ca	☐	gym	☐	art
☐	music	☐	workbook	☐	

Do I have homework?

☐ yes

☐ no ✗

Comments:

_____

_____

_____

Did I like my lunch?

☐ yummy   ☐ yucky

I ate:

_____

_____

_____

How was my mood today?

☐	happy	☐	sad	☐	frustrated

☐	okay	☐	tired	☐	grumpy

Comments:

_____

_____

_____

_____

_____

_____

_____

_____

Remember: (to take home, bring tomorrow, coming event)

_____

_____

_____

date

month / day / year

_____

What classes did I have?

☐	reading	☐	math	☐	writing
☐	spelling	☐	gym	☐	art
☐	music	☐	workbook	☐	

Do I have homework?

☐ yes

Comments:

_____

☐ no

_____

_____

Did I like my lunch?

☐ yummy   ☐ yucky

I ate:

_____

_____

_____

How was my mood today?

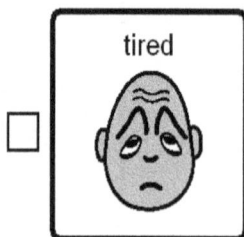

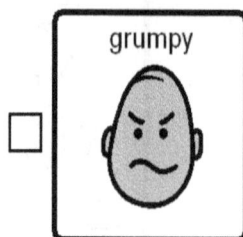

	happy		sad		frustrated
☐		☐		☐	

	okay		tired		grumpy
☐		☐		☐	

Comments:

_____

_____

_____

_____

_____

_____

_____

_____

_____

Remember: (to take home, bring tomorrow, coming event)

_____

_____

_____

_____

What classes did I have?

□ reading	□ math	□ writing
□ spelling Cat	□ gym	□ art
□ music	□ workbook	□

Do I have homework?

□ yes

□ no

Comments:

_____

_____

_____

Did I like my lunch?

□ yummy   □ yucky

I ate:

_____

_____

_____

How was my mood today?

	happy		sad		frustrated
☐		☐		☐	

	okay		tired		grumpy
☐		☐		☐	

Comments:

_____

_____

_____

_____

_____

_____

_____

_____

_____

Remember: (to take home, bring tomorrow, coming event)

_____

_____

_____

date

month / day / year

_____

What classes did I have?

☐ reading

☐ math

☐ writing

☐ spelling — Cat — Ca

☐ gym

☐ art

☐ music

☐ workbook

☐

Do I have homework?

☐ yes

☐ no

Comments:

_____

_____

_____

Did I like my lunch?

☐ yummy

☐ yucky

I ate:

_____

_____

_____

How was my mood today?

☐ happy	☐ sad	☐ frustrated
☐ okay	☐ tired	☐ grumpy

Comments:

_____

_____

_____

_____

_____

_____

_____

_____

_____

Remember: (to take home, bring tomorrow, coming event)

_____

_____

_____

date

month / day / year

_____

What classes did I have?

☐ reading

☐ math

☐ writing

☐ spelling (Cat) Ca

☐ gym

☐ art

☐ music

☐ workbook

☐

Do I have homework?

☐ yes

Comments:

_____

☐ no

_____

_____

Did I like my lunch?

☐ yummy

☐ yucky

I ate:

_____

_____

_____

How was my mood today?

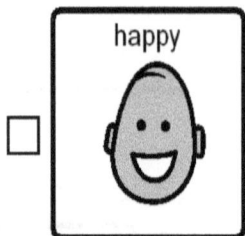

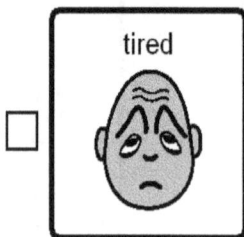

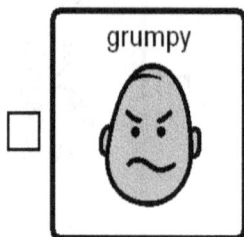

☐ happy	☐ sad	☐ frustrated
☐ okay	☐ tired	☐ grumpy

Comments:

_____

_____

_____

_____

_____

_____

_____

_____

_____

Remember: (to take home, bring tomorrow, coming event)

_____

_____

_____

date
month / day / year

_____

What classes did I have?

☐ reading	☐ math	☐ writing

☐ spelling	☐ gym	☐ art

☐ music	☐ workbook	☐

Do I have homework?

☐ yes

Comments:

_____

☐ no

_____

_____

Did I like my lunch?

☐ yummy ☐ yucky

I ate:

_____

_____

_____

How was my mood today?

	happy		sad		frustrated
☐	happy	☐	sad	☐	frustrated

	okay		tired		grumpy
☐	okay	☐	tired	☐	grumpy

Comments:

_____

_____

_____

_____

_____

_____

_____

_____

_____

Remember: (to take home, bring tomorrow, coming event)

_____

_____

_____

date

month / day / year

_____

What classes did I have?

☐ reading

☐ math
$\frac{2}{+3}$ / $\frac{3}{-2}$

☐ writing

☐ spelling
Ca Cat

☐ gym

☐ art

☐ music

☐ workbook

☐

Do I have homework?

☐ yes

Comments:
_____
_____

☐ no X

Did I like my lunch?

☐ yummy

☐ yucky

I ate:
_____
_____
_____

How was my mood today?

☐	happy
☐	sad
☐	frustrated
☐	okay
☐	tired
☐	grumpy

Comments:

_____

_____

_____

_____

_____

_____

_____

_____

_____

Remember: (to take home, bring tomorrow, coming event)

_____

_____

_____

date

month / day / year

_____

What classes did I have?

☐ reading

☐ math

☐ writing

☐ spelling — Cat / Ca

☐ gym

☐ art

☐ music

☐ workbook

☐

Do I have homework?

☐ yes

☐ no

Comments:

_____
_____
_____

Did I like my lunch?

☐ yummy

☐ yucky

I ate:

_____
_____
_____

How was my mood today?

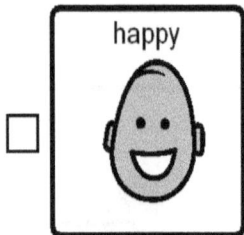

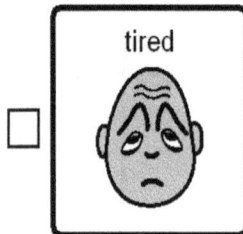

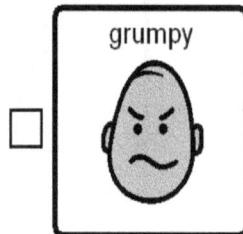

☐ happy	☐ sad	☐ frustrated
☐ okay	☐ tired	☐ grumpy

Comments:

_____

_____

_____

_____

_____

_____

_____

_____

Remember: (to take home, bring tomorrow, coming event)

_____

_____

_____

date

month / day / year

_____

What classes did I have?

☐ reading

☐ math

2
+3
___
5

3
-1
___
2

☐ writing

☐ spelling

Cat

Ca

☐ gym

☐ art

☐ music

☐ workbook

☐

Do I have homework?

☐ yes

☐ no

Comments:

_____

_____

_____

Did I like my lunch?

☐ yummy

☐ yucky

I ate:

_____

_____

_____

How was my mood today?

	happy		sad		frustrated
☐		☐		☐	

	okay		tired		grumpy
☐		☐		☐	

Comments:

_____

_____

_____

_____

_____

_____

_____

_____

_____

Remember: (to take home, bring tomorrow, coming event)

_____

_____

_____

date

month / day / year

_____

What classes did I have?

☐ reading

☐ math

☐ writing

☐ spelling — Ca "Cat"

☐ gym

☐ art

☐ music

☐ workbook

☐

Do I have homework?

☐ yes

☐ no

Comments:

_____

_____

_____

Did I like my lunch?

☐ yummy

☐ yucky

I ate:

_____

_____

_____

How was my mood today?

☐ happy	☐ sad	☐ frustrated
☐ okay	☐ tired	☐ grumpy

Comments:

_____

_____

_____

_____

_____

_____

_____

_____

Remember: (to take home, bring tomorrow, coming event)

_____

_____

_____

date

month / day / year

_____

What classes did I have?

☐ reading

☐ math

$$\begin{array}{r} 2 \\ +3 \\ \hline 5 \end{array} \qquad \begin{array}{r} 3 \\ -1 \\ \hline 2 \end{array}$$

☐ writing

☐ spelling

Cat

Ca

☐ gym

☐ art

☐ music

☐ workbook

☐

Do I have homework?

☐ yes

☐ no

Comments:

_____
_____
_____

Did I like my lunch?

☐ yummy

☐ yucky

I ate:

_____
_____
_____

How was my mood today?

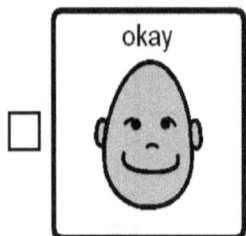

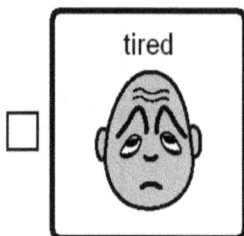

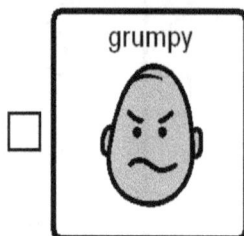

☐ happy	☐ sad	☐ frustrated
☐ okay	☐ tired	☐ grumpy

Comments:

_____

_____

_____

_____

_____

_____

_____

_____

Remember: (to take home, bring tomorrow, coming event)

_____

_____

_____

date

month / day / year

_____

What classes did I have?

☐	reading	☐	math	☐	writing

☐	spelling Cat Ca	☐	gym	☐	art

☐	music	☐	workbook	☐	

Do I have homework?

☐ yes

Comments:

_____

☐ no

_____

_____

Did I like my lunch?

I ate:

☐ yummy ☐ yucky

_____

_____

_____

How was my mood today?

☐ happy

☐ sad

☐ frustrated

☐ okay

☐ tired

☐ grumpy

Comments:

_____

_____

_____

_____

_____

_____

_____

_____

_____

Remember: (to take home, bring tomorrow, coming event)

_____

_____

_____

date

month / day / year

_____

What classes did I have?

☐ reading

☐ math

☐ writing

☐ spelling

Cat

Ca

☐ gym

☐ art

☐ music

☐ workbook

☐

Do I have homework?

☐ yes

☐ no

Comments:

_____

_____

_____

Did I like my lunch?

☐ yummy

☐ yucky

I ate:

_____

_____

_____

How was my mood today?

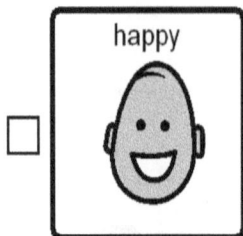

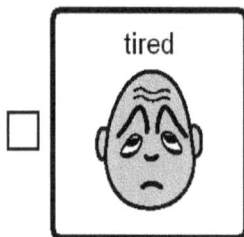

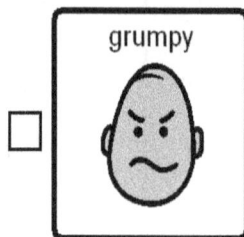

☐ happy	☐ sad	☐ frustrated
☐ okay	☐ tired	☐ grumpy

Comments:

_____

_____

_____

_____

_____

_____

_____

_____

_____

Remember: (to take home, bring tomorrow, coming event)

_____

_____

_____

date
month / day / year

_____

What classes did I have?

☐ reading

☐ math

☐ writing

☐ spelling

☐ gym

☐ art

☐ music

☐ workbook

☐

Do I have homework?

☐ yes

☐ no

Comments:

_____

_____

_____

Did I like my lunch?

☐ yummy

☐ yucky

I ate:

_____

_____

_____

How was my mood today?

☐	happy
☐	sad
☐	frustrated
☐	okay
☐	tired
☐	grumpy

Comments:

_____

_____

_____

_____

_____

_____

_____

_____

_____

Remember: (to take home, bring tomorrow, coming event)

_____

_____

_____

date

month / day / year

_____

What classes did I have?

- [ ] **reading**
- [ ] **math**
- [ ] **writing**
- [ ] **spelling** — Cat, Ca
- [ ] **gym**
- [ ] **art**
- [ ] **music**
- [ ] **workbook**
- [ ]

Do I have homework?

- [ ] yes
- [ ] no

Comments:

_____
_____
_____

Did I like my lunch?

- [ ] yummy
- [ ] yucky

I ate:

_____
_____
_____

How was my mood today?

☐ happy	☐ sad	☐ frustrated
☐ okay	☐ tired	☐ grumpy

Comments:

_____

_____

_____

_____

_____

_____

_____

_____

_____

Remember: (to take home, bring tomorrow, coming event)

_____

_____

_____

date
month / day / year

_____

What classes did I have?

☐ reading

☐ math

☐ writing

☐ spelling — Cat / Ca

☐ gym

☐ art

☐ music

☐ workbook

☐

Do I have homework?

☐ yes

☐ no

Comments:

_____

_____

_____

Did I like my lunch?

☐ yummy

☐ yucky

I ate:

_____

_____

_____

How was my mood today?

	happy		sad		frustrated
☐		☐		☐	

	okay		tired		grumpy
☐		☐		☐	

Comments:

_____

_____

_____

_____

_____

_____

_____

_____

Remember: (to take home, bring tomorrow, coming event)

_____

_____

_____

date	
month / day / year	_____

What classes did I have?

☐ reading

☐ math

☐ writing

☐ spelling — Ca / Cat

☐ gym

☐ art

☐ music

☐ workbook

☐

Do I have homework?

☐ yes

☐ no

Comments:

_____

_____

_____

Did I like my lunch?

☐ yummy

☐ yucky

I ate:

_____

_____

_____

How was my mood today?

	happy		sad		frustrated
☐		☐		☐	

	okay		tired		grumpy
☐		☐		☐	

Comments:

_____

_____

_____

_____

_____

_____

_____

_____

_____

Remember: (to take home, bring tomorrow, coming event)

_____

_____

_____

date

month / day / year

_____

What classes did I have?

☐ reading

☐ math

☐ writing

☐ spelling (Cat / Ca)

☐ gym

☐ art

☐ music

☐ workbook

☐

Do I have homework?

☐ yes

☐ no

Comments:

_____
_____
_____

Did I like my lunch?

☐ yummy

☐ yucky

I ate:

_____
_____
_____

How was my mood today?

	happy		sad		frustrated
☐		☐		☐	

	okay		tired		grumpy
☐		☐		☐	

Comments:

_____

_____

_____

_____

_____

_____

_____

_____

_____

Remember: (to take home, bring tomorrow, coming event)

_____

_____

_____

date

month / day / year

_____

What classes did I have?

☐ reading

☐ math

☐ writing

☐ spelling — Cat / Ca

☐ gym

☐ art

☐ music

☐ workbook

☐

Do I have homework?

☐ yes

☐ no

Comments:

_____

_____

_____

Did I like my lunch?

☐ yummy

☐ yucky

I ate:

_____

_____

_____

How was my mood today?

☐ happy

☐ sad

☐ frustrated

☐ okay

☐ tired

☐ grumpy

Comments:

_____

_____

_____

_____

_____

_____

_____

_____

_____

Remember: (to take home, bring tomorrow, coming event)

_____

_____

_____

date

month / day / year

_____

What classes did I have?

☐ reading

☐ math

☐ writing

☐ spelling

☐ gym

☐ art

☐ music

☐ workbook

☐

Do I have homework?

☐ yes

☐ no

Comments:

_____

_____

_____

Did I like my lunch?

☐ yummy

☐ yucky

I ate:

_____

_____

_____

How was my mood today?

| ☐ happy | ☐ sad | ☐ frustrated |
| ☐ okay | ☐ tired | ☐ grumpy |

Comments:

_____

_____

_____

_____

_____

_____

_____

_____

Remember: (to take home, bring tomorrow, coming event)

_____

_____

_____

date
month / day / year

_____

What classes did I have?

☐ reading

☐ math
$$\frac{2}{+3}{5} \quad \frac{3}{-1}{2}$$

☐ writing

☐ spelling
Ca → Cat

☐ gym

☐ art

☐ music

☐ workbook

☐

Do I have homework?

☐ yes

Comments:

_____

☐ no

_____

_____

Did I like my lunch?

I ate:

☐ yummy

☐ yucky

_____

_____

_____

How was my mood today?

	happy		sad		frustrated
☐		☐		☐	

	okay		tired		grumpy
☐		☐		☐	

Comments:

_____

_____

_____

_____

_____

_____

_____

_____

Remember: (to take home, bring tomorrow, coming event)

_____

_____

_____

date

month / day / year

_____

What classes did I have?

☐ **reading**

☐ **math**

☐ **writing**

☐ **spelling**

☐ **gym**

☐ **art**

☐ **music**

☐ **workbook**

☐

Do I have homework?

☐ **yes**

☐ **no**

Comments:

_____
_____
_____

Did I like my lunch?

☐ **yummy**

☐ **yucky**

I ate:

_____
_____
_____

How was my mood today?

☐ happy	☐ sad	☐ frustrated
☐ okay	☐ tired	☐ grumpy

Comments:

_____

_____

_____

_____

_____

_____

_____

_____

_____

Remember: (to take home, bring tomorrow, coming event)

_____

_____

_____

date

month / day / year

_____

What classes did I have?

☐ reading

☐ math

☐ writing

☐ spelling
Cat
Ca

☐ gym

☐ art

☐ music

☐ workbook

☐

Do I have homework?

☐ yes

Comments:

_____

☐ no

_____

_____

Did I like my lunch?

I ate:

☐ yummy

☐ yucky

_____

_____

_____

How was my mood today?

	happy		sad		frustrated
☐		☐		☐	

	okay		tired		grumpy
☐		☐		☐	

Comments:

_____

_____

_____

_____

_____

_____

_____

_____

Remember: (to take home, bring tomorrow, coming event)

_____

_____

_____

date

month / day / year

_____

What classes did I have?

☐ reading	☐ math	☐ writing
☐ spelling Cat Ca	☐ gym	☐ art
☐ music	☐ workbook	☐

Do I have homework?

☐ yes

☐ no

Comments:

_____
_____
_____

Did I like my lunch?

☐ yummy   ☐ yucky

I ate:

_____
_____
_____

How was my mood today?

☐ happy

☐ sad

☐ frustrated

☐ okay

☐ tired

☐ grumpy

Comments:

_____

_____

_____

_____

_____

_____

_____

_____

Remember: (to take home, bring tomorrow, coming event)

_____

_____

_____

date

month / day / year

_____

What classes did I have?

☐ reading

☐ math

☐ writing

☐ spelling
Ca Cat

☐ gym

☐ art

☐ music

☐ workbook

☐

Do I have homework?

☐ yes

Comments:

_____

☐ no

_____

_____

Did I like my lunch?

I ate:

☐ yummy

☐ yucky

_____

_____

_____

How was my mood today?

☐ happy	☐ sad	☐ frustrated
☐ okay	☐ tired	☐ grumpy

Comments:

_____

_____

_____

_____

_____

_____

_____

_____

Remember: (to take home, bring tomorrow, coming event)

_____

_____

_____

date

month / day / year

_____

What classes did I have?

☐ reading

☐ math

☐ writing

☐ spelling
Cat
Ca

☐ gym

☐ art

☐ music

☐ workbook

☐

Do I have homework?

☐ yes

☐ no

Comments:

_____

_____

_____

Did I like my lunch?

☐ yummy

☐ yucky

I ate:

_____

_____

_____

How was my mood today?

☐ happy

☐ sad

☐ frustrated

☐ okay

☐ tired

☐ grumpy

Comments:

_____

_____

_____

_____

_____

_____

_____

_____

_____

Remember: (to take home, bring tomorrow, coming event)

_____

_____

_____

date

month / day / year

_____

What classes did I have?

☐ reading

☐ math

☐ writing

☐ spelling — Cat / Ca

☐ gym

☐ art

☐ music

☐ workbook

☐

Do I have homework?

☐ yes

☐ no

Comments:

_____
_____
_____

Did I like my lunch?

☐ yummy

☐ yucky

I ate:

_____
_____
_____

How was my mood today?

☐ happy	☐ sad	☐ frustrated
☐ okay	☐ tired	☐ grumpy

Comments:

_____

_____

_____

_____

_____

_____

_____

_____

Remember: (to take home, bring tomorrow, coming event)

_____

_____

_____

date

month / day / year

_____

What classes did I have?

☐ reading

☐ math
2
+3
—
5

3
−1
—
2

☐ writing

☐ spelling
Cat
Ca

☐ gym

☐ art

☐ music

☐ workbook

☐

Do I have homework?

☐ yes

☐ no

Comments:

_____

_____

_____

Did I like my lunch?

☐ yummy

☐ yucky

I ate:

_____

_____

_____

How was my mood today?

☐ happy	☐ sad	☐ frustrated
☐ okay	☐ tired	☐ grumpy

Comments:

_____

_____

_____

_____

_____

_____

_____

_____

_____

Remember: (to take home, bring tomorrow, coming event)

_____

_____

_____

date

month / day / year

_____

What classes did I have?

☐ reading

☐ math

☐ writing

☐ spelling

☐ gym

☐ art

☐ music

☐ workbook

☐

Do I have homework?

☐ yes

☐ no

Comments:

_____

_____

_____

Did I like my lunch?

☐ yummy

☐ yucky

I ate:

_____

_____

_____

How was my mood today?

☐ happy	☐ sad	☐ frustrated
☐ okay	☐ tired	☐ grumpy

Comments:

_____

_____

_____

_____

_____

_____

_____

_____

Remember: (to take home, bring tomorrow, coming event)

_____

_____

_____

date

month / day / year

_____

What classes did I have?

☐ reading

☐ math

☐ writing

☐ spelling — Cat / Ca

☐ gym

☐ art

☐ music

☐ workbook

☐

Do I have homework?

☐ yes

☐ no

Comments:

_____

_____

_____

Did I like my lunch?

☐ yummy

☐ yucky

I ate:

_____

_____

_____

How was my mood today?

☐ happy	☐ sad	☐ frustrated
☐ okay	☐ tired	☐ grumpy

Comments:

_____

_____

_____

_____

_____

_____

_____

_____

Remember: (to take home, bring tomorrow, coming event)

_____

_____

_____

date

month / day / year

_____

What classes did I have?

☐ **reading**

☐ **math**
2
+3
___
5

3
-1
___
2

☐ **writing**

☐ **spelling**
Cat
Ca

☐ **gym**

☐ **art**

☐ **music**

☐ **workbook**

☐

Do I have homework?

☐ **yes**

☐ **no** X

Comments:

_____

_____

_____

Did I like my lunch?

☐ **yummy**

☐ **yucky**

I ate:

_____

_____

_____

How was my mood today?

☐ happy	☐ sad	☐ frustrated
☐ okay	☐ tired	☐ grumpy

Comments:

_____

_____

_____

_____

_____

_____

_____

_____

_____

Remember: (to take home, bring tomorrow, coming event)

_____

_____

_____

date

month / day / year

_____

What classes did I have?

☐ reading

☐ math

☐ writing

☐ spelling (Ca → Cat)

☐ gym

☐ art

☐ music

☐ workbook

☐

Do I have homework?

☐ yes

☐ no

Comments:

_____

_____

_____

Did I like my lunch?

☐ yummy

☐ yucky

I ate:

_____

_____

_____

How was my mood today?

- [ ] happy
- [ ] sad
- [ ] frustrated
- [ ] okay
- [ ] tired
- [ ] grumpy

Comments:

_____

_____

_____

_____

_____

_____

_____

_____

Remember: (to take home, bring tomorrow, coming event)

_____

_____

_____

date

month / day / year

_____

What classes did I have?

☐ reading

☐ math

☐ writing

☐ spelling

☐ gym

☐ art

☐ music

☐ workbook

☐

Do I have homework?

☐ yes

☐ no

Comments:

_____

_____

_____

Did I like my lunch?

☐ yummy

☐ yucky

I ate:

_____

_____

_____

How was my mood today?

☐	happy	☐	sad	☐	frustrated

☐	okay	☐	tired	☐	grumpy

Comments:

_____

_____

_____

_____

_____

_____

_____

_____

Remember: (to take home, bring tomorrow, coming event)

_____

_____

_____

date

month / day / year

_____

What classes did I have?

☐ **reading**

☐ **math**
$$\begin{array}{r} 2 \\ +3 \\ \hline 5 \end{array} \qquad \begin{array}{r} 3 \\ -1 \\ \hline 2 \end{array}$$

☐ **writing**

☐ **spelling**
Ca — Cat

☐ **gym**

☐ **art**

☐ **music**

☐ **workbook**

☐

Do I have homework?

☐ **yes**

☐ **no**

Comments:

_____

_____

_____

Did I like my lunch?

☐ **yummy**

☐ **yucky**

I ate:

_____

_____

_____

How was my mood today?

☐ happy	☐ sad	☐ frustrated
☐ okay	☐ tired	☐ grumpy

Comments:

_____

_____

_____

_____

_____

_____

_____

_____

_____

Remember: (to take home, bring tomorrow, coming event)

_____

_____

_____

date
month / day / year

_____

What classes did I have?

☐ reading	☐ math	☐ writing

☐ spelling	☐ gym	☐ art

☐ music	☐ workbook	☐

Do I have homework?

☐ yes

☐ no

Comments:

_____

_____

_____

Did I like my lunch?

☐ yummy ☐ yucky

I ate:

_____

_____

_____

How was my mood today?

	happy		sad		frustrated
☐	😃	☐	😢	☐	😖

	okay		tired		grumpy
☐	🙂	☐	😫	☐	😠

Comments:

_____

_____

_____

_____

_____

_____

_____

_____

Remember: (to take home, bring tomorrow, coming event)

_____

_____

_____

date

month / day / year

_____

What classes did I have?

☐ reading

☐ math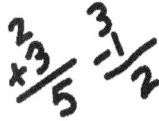

☐ writing

☐ spelling

☐ gym

☐ art

☐ music

☐ workbook

☐

Do I have homework?

☐ yes

Comments:

_____

☐ no

_____

_____

Did I like my lunch?

☐ yummy  ☐ yucky

I ate:

_____

_____

_____

How was my mood today?

☐ happy	☐ sad	☐ frustrated
☐ okay	☐ tired	☐ grumpy

Comments:

_____

_____

_____

_____

_____

_____

_____

_____

Remember: (to take home, bring tomorrow, coming event)

_____

_____

_____

_____

What classes did I have?

☐ reading

☐ math

☐ writing

☐ spelling

☐ gym

☐ art

☐ music

☐ workbook

☐

Do I have homework?

☐ yes

Comments:

_____

☐ no

_____

_____

Did I like my lunch?

I ate:

☐ yummy

☐ yucky

_____

_____

_____

How was my mood today?

☐ happy	☐ sad	☐ frustrated
☐ okay	☐ tired	☐ grumpy

Comments:

_____

_____

_____

_____

_____

_____

_____

_____

_____

Remember: (to take home, bring tomorrow, coming event)

_____

_____

_____

date

month / day / year

_____

What classes did I have?

☐	**reading**
☐	**math**
☐	**writing**
☐	**spelling** Ca Cat
☐	**gym**
☐	**art**
☐	**music**
☐	**workbook**
☐	

Do I have homework?

☐ yes

Comments:

_____

☐ no

_____

_____

Did I like my lunch?

☐ **yummy**

☐ **yucky**

I ate:

_____

_____

_____

How was my mood today?

☐ happy	☐ sad	☐ frustrated
☐ okay	☐ tired	☐ grumpy

Comments:

_____

_____

_____

_____

_____

_____

_____

_____

_____

Remember: (to take home, bring tomorrow, coming event)

_____

_____

_____

date

month / day / year

_____

What classes did I have?

☐ reading

☐ math

$$\frac{\begin{array}{r}2\\+3\end{array}}{5} \quad \frac{\begin{array}{r}3\\-1\end{array}}{2}$$

☐ writing

☐ spelling

Cat

Ca

☐ gym

☐ art

☐ music

☐ workbook

☐

Do I have homework?

☐ yes

Comments:

_____

☐ no

_____

_____

Did I like my lunch?

I ate:

☐ yummy

☐ yucky

_____

_____

_____

How was my mood today?

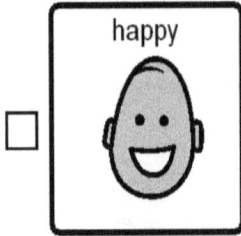

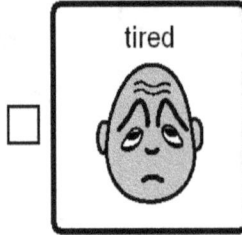

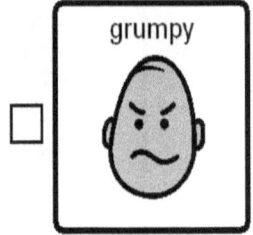

☐ happy	☐ sad	☐ frustrated
☐ okay	☐ tired	☐ grumpy

Comments:

_____

_____

_____

_____

_____

_____

_____

_____

_____

Remember: (to take home, bring tomorrow, coming event)

_____

_____

_____

date
month / day / year

_____

What classes did I have?

☐ reading

☐ math

☐ writing

☐ spelling — Ca — Cat

☐ gym

☐ art

☐ music

☐ workbook

☐

Do I have homework?

☐ yes

☐ no

Comments:
_____
_____
_____

Did I like my lunch?

☐ yummy

☐ yucky

I ate:
_____
_____
_____

How was my mood today?

	happy		sad		frustrated
☐		☐		☐	

	okay		tired		grumpy
☐		☐		☐	

Comments:

_____

_____

_____

_____

_____

_____

_____

_____

Remember: (to take home, bring tomorrow, coming event)

_____

_____

_____

date

month / day / year

_____

What classes did I have?

☐ reading

☐ math

☐ writing

☐ spelling

☐ gym

☐ art

☐ music

☐ workbook

☐

Do I have homework?

☐ yes

Comments:

_____

☐ no

_____

_____

Did I like my lunch?

☐ yummy

☐ yucky

I ate:

_____

_____

_____

How was my mood today?

☐ happy	☐ sad	☐ frustrated
☐ okay	☐ tired	☐ grumpy

Comments:

_____

_____

_____

_____

_____

_____

_____

_____

_____

Remember: (to take home, bring tomorrow, coming event)

_____

_____

_____

date

month / day / year

_____

What classes did I have?

☐ reading

☐ math

☐ writing

☐ spelling
Ca Cat

☐ gym

☐ art

☐ music

☐ workbook

☐

Do I have homework?

☐ yes

☐ no

Comments:

_____
_____
_____

Did I like my lunch?

☐ yummy

☐ yucky

I ate:

_____
_____
_____

How was my mood today?

☐ happy	☐ sad	☐ frustrated
☐ okay	☐ tired	☐ grumpy

Comments:

_____

_____

_____

_____

_____

_____

_____

_____

Remember: (to take home, bring tomorrow, coming event)

_____

_____

_____

Notes:

_____

_____

_____

_____

_____

_____

_____

_____

_____

_____

_____

_____

_____

_____

_____

_____

_____

_____

_____

_____

_____

www.ingramcontent.com/pod-product-compliance
Lightning Source LLC
Chambersburg PA
CBHW020654270326
41928CB00005B/117